T0146997

# OUR EMERGING WORLD

# OUR EMERGING WORLD

## POLITICS, ECONOMICS, CULTURE, ENVIRONMENT, AND THE NEW RENAISSANCE

### GIOVANNI BURRASCANO

# OUR EMERGING WORLD
## POLITICS, ECONOMICS, CULTURE, ENVIRONMENT, AND THE NEW RENAISSANCE

iUniverse books may be ordered through booksellers or by contacting:

iUniverse
1663 Liberty Drive
Bloomington, IN 47403
www.iuniverse.com
1-800-Authors (1-800-288-4677)

ISBN: 978-1-5320-5887-5 (sc)
ISBN: 978-1-5320-5889-9 (hc)
ISBN: 978-1-5320-5888-2 (e)

Library of Congress Control Number: 2018911943

Print information available on the last page.

iUniverse rev. date: 02/26/2019

# CONTENTS

To our living earth and its peoples

# PREFACE

The publication of my first book in 2016 was truly thrilling, and I am equally excited about the present essay, which I sculpted with care and passion. I hope the subject dazzles and inspires readers as much as it has me.

After I had completed and reviewed a draft of this book, a question lingered in my mind. For some time, I kept asking myself what modern-day, single-most-important event contributed to shaping our present world's political-economic, global, sociocultural, and environmental circumstances. After I reflected on the matter, it hit me like thunder—President Nixon's trip to China in the seventies.

In 1968, Nixon defeated Democrat Hubert Humphrey in a close race and became the thirty-seventh president of the United States. His presidency lasted from 1969 to 1974. That was a time when, in 1969, the Apollo 11 spacecraft allowed humans to walk on the moon for the first time. In 1970, the Beatles broke up. In 1971, the Walt Disney theme park opened its doors, and the videocassette recorder and the microprocessor for computing were introduced.

In 1972, the world was still in the Cold War with no end in sight, the Watergate scandal began, team Canada won the unforgettable Canada-Russia hockey Summit Series, and pocket-size calculators became a reality. In 1973, the Supreme Court made abortion legal in the United States, American troops were withdrawn from Vietnam, and the oil crisis caused dramatic worldwide inflation and an economic slowdown. It was also the year the mobile telephone was invented. In 1974, smaller, digital-based consumer products began to appear in retail outlets. Because of the Watergate scandal, President Nixon stepped down halfway through his second term to become the first American president forced to resign from office.

This brief section concerning Nixon's trip to China is important in terms of its place in history and to this study, as it is the cornerstone of my argument for this book. We are today comprehending the direct effects of Nixon's foreign policy decisions of the early seventies that set the stage for what became global politics, economics, culture, and the environment. Many historical and contemporary reasons created and sustained global economic growth, but the continual expansion of today's global economy, globalization, and cultural and environmental issues have important roots in the Nixon presidency.

During the 1970s, the news coverage of the Cold War, the Vietnam War, the presidency of Richard Nixon, his visit to China, and the notorious Watergate scandal was huge. I was nine or ten at the time, and though I was interested in the facts and sometimes disturbing pictures the media were presenting, I didn't always comprehend the context, connotations, and importance of what I was seeing and hearing; these were very complicated issues to begin with.

I recall the extensive television news coverage of Nixon's trip to China. The moment I found the answer to my question above, I was not certain of the exact year Nixon's trip had taken place, and until very recently, I thought the purpose of the trip had been solely to open a new economic market for the United States. But as I read more on the matter, I learned that the trip to China had occurred in February 1972 and had taken place for many reasons.

Nixon's trip to China was a strategic attempt to improve relations with the Soviet Union in hopes of resolving the Vietnam War. China and the Soviet Union were providing behind-the-scenes military support with jets, tanks, ammunition, surface-to-air missiles, know-how in warfare, and moral support to communist North Vietnam. The US was backing the noncommunist South Vietnamese in a similar fashion to stop the spread of communism throughout Southeast Asia.

Nixon's visit to China was a strategic move on the global political chessboard. He thought that being on good terms with the most populous nation in the world and a potentially very strong country was better than having that nation eventually grow in global power but despise America and the West. He also didn't want to see China strengthen ties with Russia and become a formidable world power in the spread of communism.

As such, the visit was also designed to drive a wedge between China and the Soviet Union. He also believed improvement in Sino-American relations was an instrument of peace. When the Soviets understood that there was a real possibility China would become closer to the United States, the idea of having friendlier relations with America appealed to the Russians. They could not fathom a scenario in which China became closely aligned with the US and form a union that posed a threat to Soviet security worldwide. America's new openness to China, therefore, led to reduced tensions with the Soviets.

The Vietnam War commenced in 1955, and the US was involved from the outset providing various forms of support, including financial and military assistance. However, it was at the beginning of March, 1965, that the US adopted a militarily combative role in the war because it had become clear that the American-backed French army in South Vietnam was very close to losing the battle against communist forces. To help South Vietnam, on March 8, 1965, the first wave of 3500 US Marines came ashore at China Beach north of Da Nang. Casualties were very high, and the American public had had enough of the war. By the fall of 1972, the Nixon administration was confronted with severe public pressure to withdraw from the war. Diplomatically, US efforts to align itself with China and the Soviet Union were designed to pressure North Vietnam into seeking a settlement that would end the conflict. The US sought to persuade the Soviets and Chinese to convince the North Vietnamese to seriously negotiate and reach an agreement to end the war. The two countries did not do so in a direct fashion, but both indirectly contributed to finding a resolution.

Li and Hong (1998, 403) state that the Chinese leaders would not agree to provide direct help in resolving the Vietnam conflict and did not pressure Hanoi to do so but did not hinder American efforts to negotiate a settlement.

The Soviets refused to exert direct pressure on the North Vietnamese but acted as a message carrier between America and North Vietnam. Gaiduk (in Stanke 1998) enumerates the Soviet reasons for wanting an end to the war. The Soviets had been seeking a negotiated peace settlement between the US and North Vietnam between 1965 and 1967, attempting to bring both sides to the negotiating table. The Soviets were eager to end the war in Vietnam, but it also had to serve their objectives— first, Soviet leadership did not want the war to escalate to a nuclear war, nor did it want to be forced into a confrontation with the US. Second, the Soviets wanted to impede China's influence in Southeast Asia and the communist world. Third, the Soviets thought that a very elongated war would diminish the prospects of détente with the United States.

The Soviets feared direct pressure on North Vietnam could cause Hanoi to draw closer to the Chinese. Hence, the Soviets involved themselves only by acting as a third party between the Americans and North Vietnamese, relaying information regarding possible concessions, positions on matters, and proposals that might allow talks to start.

By March 1968, Soviet diplomacy helped the North Vietnamese and Americans come to the negotiation table and open preliminary talks under President Johnson's administration, but the talks went nowhere. The Soviets continuously did all they could to keep the warring parties at the table, and they provided a temporary direct contribution with the design and provision of compromises for consideration by both sides. The Soviets soon reverted to their role as message carrier.

Nixon elevated efforts to obtain Soviet involvement and cooperation in the quest of a peaceful resolution to the war. Soviet involvement led to the Paris Peace talks in January 1969 and continued to play a strategic role at the Paris talks after Nixon won his first election (Hershberg 1996, 256). The Soviets, therefore, without forcing Hanoi directly to end the war, made important contributions to peace negotiations that eventually led to the signing of the Paris Peace Accord in January 1973. They did in fact provide more eager and active assistance than did China in facilitating an end to the war and fulfilled their country's primary objectives. A secondary effect of the Soviet effort was that it allowed the United States to withdraw from the war.

The Paris Peace talks did not always proceed smoothly. Private negotiations between US national security adviser Henry Kissinger and the North Vietnamese leadership had produced no results by December 13, 1972, when peace talks collapsed. Nixon was extremely angered by that because he wanted to end the war quickly in order to stop the death and injury of American soldiers, to put an end to the Vietnam anti-war protest, to no longer financially invest in the costly war totaling $168 billion between 1953 and 1975 for the US, to fulfill a crucial electoral promise made during his 1968 electoral campaign pledging to end the war, and to prepare the groundwork as part of his political platform for his next electoral campaign in which he could tell the American electorate that his presidency successfully ended the war. In relation to this, a matter that heavily preoccupied the president was his fear that the new upcoming 93rd Congress would legislate an end to the war, disallowing him from ending it on his terms and declaring its end. He also wanted peace in Southeast Asia and the world but for many years it was speculated, and, more recent information suggests, that Nixon extended the duration of the war for political gain. This is one example of why he was awarded the derogatory nickname "Tricky Dicky"; Schultz (2013) describes how in 1968, the Paris Peace talks initially failed because a close assistant to the then-Presidential candidate Richard Nixon convinced the South Vietnamese to abandon and stall the talks conveying that, if elected, the Nixon administration would offer a much better deal. Nixon feared that if a negotiated settlement to the war was achieved, it would derail his campaign based on a political platform that was against the war. Hence, in order to win the election, he needed continuation of the war.

What eventually brought the North Vietnamese to sign a cease-fire agreement? Thinking that the Soviets and Chinese had sided with the United States, the North Vietnamese felt abandoned by China and the Soviet Union—they were now isolated and left to fend for themselves in the war. In addition, the Chinese significantly reduced the supply of military materials to the North Vietnamese, and the United States strategically cut off Soviet military assistance to them by interdicting logistics routes to North Vietnam resulting in very small quantities of military supplies reaching the North Vietnamese. The North Vietnamese were left with an anemic amount of military might to continue their war.

At the same time, the result of Nixon's fury was felt between December 18 and December 29, 1972, when the US, in what is known as the Christmas Bombing of operation Linebacker II, unleashed a relentless, B-52 aircraft heavy bombardment of Haiphong, and especially of Hanoi, in an attempt to force the North Vietnamese back to the negotiating table.

At that point, the North Vietnamese were essentially brought to their knees. In the words of Henry Kissinger, "We bombed the North Vietnamese into accepting our concessions." Lack of military supplies and constant American bombardment brought the North Vietnamese back to resume peace talks, and the Paris Peace Accord was signed by all concerned parties on January 27, 1973. That ended the US commitment to the Vietnam War and permitted the withdrawal of American troops from Vietnam that year.

The accord represented a cease-fire between North and South Vietnam. Though the spirit of the agreement called for each party to not wage war upon each other, very important clashes did occur, instigated primarily by North Vietnam, as neither the Soviets nor the North Vietnamese abided by the accord's provisions.

As American troops were being withdrawn, the war continued. After the reduction of military supplies and US bombardment of Haiphong and Hanoi, battered North Vietnamese military forces managed to slowly strengthen their military infrastructure over the two years following the Paris Peace Accord.

By April 1975, the North Vietnamese were sufficiently robust to launch a decisive military assault on the South Vietnamese, capture Saigon, and win the war. Though the United States assured military and other strategic support to the South Vietnamese during the Paris Peace Accord negotiation process in case the North Vietnamese attacked, such help was never provided. By the time the decisive assault took place, Nixon was absorbed in and distracted by the Watergate scandal and later forced from office. America had already withdrawn much of its troops and military infrastructure from the region, there were domestic economic constraints, and new American governmental policy no longer allowed the provisioning of military assistance to South Vietnam.

Nixon's visit to China led to American diplomatic relations with the Soviet Union and a thawing of the Cold War between the two countries with détente. The process began with key concessions made by the Soviets. The period of détente lasted between the late 1960s and late 1970s. The concessions made were signed agreements between Nixon and the secretary general of the Soviet Communist party, Leonid I. Brezhnev, during a planned post-China visit by Nixon to Moscow in May 1972. It was deemed in the best interest of both countries if commercial trade was increased and the danger posed by potential nuclear warfare was reduced.

Several important agreements were signed at this first summit, among them the first Strategic Arms Limitation Treaty dealing with limitations on nuclear capabilities and on antiballistic missile weaponry for both superpowers. This included disarmament of biological weaponry. There was also an agreement concerning cooperation between the two countries regarding research in a variety of fields, including space exploration and another agreement aimed at increasing commercial trade ties. The two sides signed an agreement regarding the sale of US grain to the Soviets.

Two subsequent similar summits that took place in 1973 and 1974 produced important but generally lesser results. By the end of the 1970s, certain events, in particular the Soviet stance on human rights and its 1979 invasion of Afghanistan, caused friction and cooled relations between the two superpowers. Détente came to a gradual end through the subsequent presidencies of Jimmy Carter and Ronald Reagan.

To Nixon's dislike and frustration, improved US relations with the Soviet Union and China drove Western European nations to seek political and economic unity. Siracusa and Nguyen (2018, 115–25) say that during the Nixon presidency, America shifted its foreign policy attention from building a strong post–World War II Western Europe so it could thrive economically and have sufficient weight to stave off Soviet expansionism and its attempts to build a stronger Eastern Europe.

The Western European community's response was that it felt it had the right to have its unified political voice heard concerning international affairs. Nixon worried that Western European community political cooperation and greater clout could upset his foreign policy objectives with China and the Soviets. He also perceived Western European political cooperation as competition to America's leadership position in the West.

Aside from the goal of ending the Vietnam War, a crucial reason Nixon reached out to China and the Soviet Union was the realization that overall, America and its economy were in serious decline and that having closer trade ties with large developing communist markets could improve the US economically. Western European community leaders embraced the prospect of reduced East-West Cold War tensions because they acknowledged there would be significantly less of a propensity for nuclear war above European territory between the superpowers and the potential for themselves to participate economically in the communist Chinese marketplace.

More important for Nixon, however, was that he sought better relations with China at a moment when support for his administration was low domestically and internationally. That was due particularly to the unpopular and frustrating Vietnam War, the 1973 oil crisis and closely associated lackluster economic performance at home, and often violent domestic social unrest stemming from protest movements. The protests were inspired by the successes of movements in the 1960s, including the black civil rights movement, the women's movement, the Native American movement, the environmental movement, the gay and lesbian movement, the white student movement that alongside blacks fought racism and poverty, and the Vietnam antiwar movement.

The visit to China provided good media coverage and political publicity in the West, and Nixon's approval ratings improved; he had a post-China-visit approval rating of 56 percent in March 1972 compared to a 49 percent in January 1972 (Gallup 1972). Nixon went on to a second term as president on November 7, 1972, defeating Democrat George McGovern in a landslide.

Nixon's visit to China forty-six years ago laid the foundation that helped shape today's global economic situation and paved the way for China's debut on the world stage as a global power. China's introduction to the global economy opened it to the West. At that time, Nixon himself understood the significance of this seven-day official visit by stating, "This was the week that changed the world" (Ignatius 2012). This historic trip is considered by historians, scholars, and journalists as one of the most important, if not the most important, visits by an American president to any part of the globe. Political, economic, sociocultural, and environmental repercussions of the Nixon visit continue to this day.

The seven-day visit to China, February 21–28, 1972, was a rapprochement that ended twenty-five years of no communication and no diplomatic relations between the two nations and was a pivotal moment in progressing toward normalization of relations between them. Thornton (1982, 355–56) says that strategically, communist China felt the need to align itself with the United States to counterbalance growing Soviet power and assertiveness as well as to resolve the Vietnam War.

Such an alignment would benefit the US and China because in subtle ways, China would aid in the withdrawal of American troops from Southeast Asia. China thought that would help deter possible Soviet aggression. China's chairman Mao Zedong viewed the Soviets with suspicion and was constantly worried about Soviet territorial expansionist intentions. He feared military and nuclear war particularly because of the Soviet invasion of Czechoslovakia in 1968 and bloody clashes at different Russian-Chinese border spots.

In 1969, the Soviet leadership in fact did threaten China with bombardment of its early-stage nuclear facilities. Mao's distrust, fear, and uncertainty caused him to want another ally in its increasingly tense and soured relationship with the Soviet Union; he thought that closer ties with America might serve as a deterrent to the Soviets. China's and the US's perception of the Soviet Union as a threat brought the two countries closer and gave them a common and bonding concern for the future.

Mao also needed to bring China out of international isolation due to the social and economic ravages of the failed 1958 Great Leap Forward, which attempted to shift its economy away from agricultural production and toward rapid industrialization; that caused famine and according to Schaeffer (2009, 181–84) the death of between fourteen million and twenty-six million people until 1961.

Mao sought major social change beginning in 1966 with the Chinese Cultural Revolution characterized as Mao-approved mass chaos unleashed by his Red Guard to expose and cleanse the Chinese Communist Party of his enemies, essentially anyone who appeared to support capitalism and traditional elements, from Chinese society. He sought to preserve the pristine nature of the communist ideology in the party and in wider Chinese society by a massive and often violent purging of people and any symbolic remnants of capitalism and traditional societal characteristics.

Mao welcomed the possibility of increased trade with the US because though the revolution may have attained some semblance of its ideological goal, it had left the country in economic shambles, societal distress, and exhaustion. Mao realized that for his new ambitions to materialize and to establish diplomatic ties with the US, he had to end China's international isolation. On the eve of Nixon's first term, the isolation did end. At that crucial point, the communist dictatorship received much-needed assistance from the US as the Chinese regime allowed itself to obtain foreign loans for investment in industry. Trade was also allowed, and the Chinese regime opened itself to foreign investment in the development of industries. China's approach was the application of reforms based on communism that used capitalism to achieve the country's aspirations.

Chang (2015, 223–27) explains that in the minds of the Chinese leadership, Moscow, not Washington, was at that point considered the greater threat. Beginning in the late 1960s, behind-the-scenes communiqués and informal meetings set the stage for a rekindling of US-China relations, and by 1971 China and the United States were signaling to each other that the time for change had arrived and a dialogue with one another needed to take place. In the absence of regular, direct, high-level, political communication, interpretation of these signals was extremely difficult for each country. Subtle messages were sent through televised speeches or through messages via other nation governmental officials, newspapers, and media photos, but the messages were either not received or not clear.

Fatefully, a favorite Chinese sport—Ping-Pong, to be exact—became the springboard that launched diplomatic talks between the two nations, now called Ping-Pong diplomacy. In April 1971, American

Ping-Pong players arrive in Nagoya, Japan, to partake in the World Table Tennis Championships. Team USA player Glenn Cowan missed the bus that was to take him to his hotel. Chinese team leader Zhang Zedong took notice and invited Cowan to board the Chinese team bus that was headed for the hotel. While on the bus, Zedong presented Cowan with a richly woven and embossed silk cloth depicting the Huangshan Mountains. The next day, Cowan reciprocated the kind gesture and presented Zedong with a red-white-and-blue T-shirt that had the peace sign and the words *Let It Be* on it.

Chairman Mao read about this gift exchange and used the friendly acts by the Chinese and American players to his diplomatic advantage. During that time, Mao was considering distancing China from its neighbor to the north, the Soviet Union, and other geographically close, neighboring, hostile republics and countries directly aligned with or sympathetic to the USSR—Mongolia, Kazakhstan, Kyrgyzstan, Tajikistan, Uzbekistan, Turkmenistan, Afghanistan, North Korea, North Vietnam, Laos, and Cambodia. It was the moment he desired to take his country out of isolation. To achieve these ends, he wanted to align with the United States.

Wanting to signal his intent to the Soviets and neighboring hostile countries of his possible shift in alliance, he asked his foreign ministry to invite the American players on an all-expenses-paid visit to China that would make them the first Americans to visit since the communist takeover in 1949. It was an unexpected invitation. The American team arrived in the People's Republic of China on April 10, 1971, and the US team later invited the Chinese team to the United States. The Chinese players set foot in Detroit on April 12, 1972, for a series of matches held in several cities across the US (Andrews 2016).

Nixon's political intuition caused him to suspect that China wanted to be reached out to, and he was correct. Acknowledging Mao's gesture of openness to the American table tennis team, on April 14, 1971, the new Nixon administration eased trade and travel restrictions to China that had been in place for twenty years.

After the US table tennis team arrived home, Nixon did not want to lose momentum. He secretly sent national security adviser Henry Kissinger on a first diplomatic mission to Beijing in July 1971 to meet with Premier Zhou En-Lai. This mission ultimately laid the groundwork that allowed Nixon to visit China the following year. Feeling less threatened by the Americans, China became receptive to Nixon's extension of an olive branch. Knowing Nixon's desire to visit China, Premier En-Lai, on behalf of the government of the People's Republic of China, invited him to China.

Nixon set foot on Chinese soil in Beijing on February 21, 1972, the first US president to visit the People's Republic of China since the communists had seized political power in 1949. There had been no American-Chinese relations since 1949, when China became a communist state. Until 1972, communist China had largely isolated itself from the world and was not aligned with any major global power. It was in fact an enemy of the United States and the Soviet Union. China was at odds with the US because it supported noncommunist South Korea during the Korean War that took place between June, 1950 and July, 1953, when an armistice was signed. The US became involved in this war in order to impede the spread of communism on the Korean peninsula and prevent a domino effect that could cause other nations in Southeastern Asia to become communist. China was also at odds with the Soviet Union, even though both countries provided direct support to communist North Korea during the war. Mao felt letdown by Soviet leader Nikita Khrushchev because he thought the Soviets could have mobilized much more Russian troops to fight alongside the Chinese. He also felt embarrassed because the Soviets requested payment from China for all the military materials supplied. In addition, the Soviets often had a condescending attitude toward China's military regarding the improper training of Chinese soldiers and the quality of military equipment they used. These factors eventually contributed to the Sino-Soviet split when China broke diplomatic relations with the Soviet Union in 1960. China ventured in a new direction wanting to be self-reliant. The key reason for the China-Soviet split, however, was ideological disagreement over the type of communism to support and spread worldwide. It was also about which leader of these two large communist powers was to take the helm in international communism. Ideologically, the Soviet view of communism was one of peaceful coexistence with the capitalist West. For China's Mao, however, his ideology of communism was pugnacious, aggressive, and given to waging war upon capitalist countries. This, according to the Soviets, was a very dangerous attitude and ideology, especially, because the Soviets wanted to reduce the risk of nuclear war with the United States. The China-Soviet split lasted between 1956 and 1966. By the 1970s, China was still politically isolated by the US and Soviet Union, as well as their respective allies, and transacted virtually no foreign trade.

Nixon's visit was a very important event because the United States sought better relations with a communist state during the Cold War. Nixon visited three Chinese cities—Beijing, Hangzhou, and Shanghai. He met with Chairman Mao Zedong and Premier Zhou En-Lai and other high-ranking Chinese officials. It was agreed that both nations would pursue cultural and economic ties with one another. Nixon, a staunch anticommunist and believer of the Keynesian trickle-down economic model, thought that this was fantastic because it promised to generate wealth for the American economy.

Historically, China was one of the great civilizations of the world possessing a very advanced and sophisticated culture. In regard to science and technology alone, China was ahead of the Western world from early times and into the Middle Ages.

According to Chang (2015, 9–10), a thousand years before the early 1800s, China's economy was in all probability the most prosperous in the world until the unexpected and amazing rise of the Atlantic world and the ascendancy of Europe over the rest of the world from 1800 to 1950 (Europe's economic rise occurred between 1500 and 1800).

Without the Nixon visit, modern-day China might well have developed, but it might have taken a different course and decades more for that to happen. The fact that Nixon visited the country accelerated the development process and made dealing with the West possible and focal to the country's spectacular economic rise since the seventies. It happened in a newly realigned global balance of power in which the American presence and relationship with China fended off possible Soviet threats and allowed China to effectively focus on its development, especially after the death of Mao in 1976.

After Mao's death, Deng Xiaoping, an important leader of the People's Republic of China (1978–1989) launched and spearheaded profound economic reforms that enhanced China's opening to the global economy while never having held high offices such as head of state or general secretary. Today, the US has an open-trade policy with China, and both countries benefit from cultural and economic ties. In fact, Morrison (2018, 2) reports that in 1980, US-China trade (exports plus imports) totaled approximately $4 billion. By 2017, this figure climbed to $636 billion, making China the USA's biggest trading partner.

Western countries have acknowledged China's importance in the world's political-economic order. The country rapidly pulled itself out of the unfortunate social and economic circumstances of the Cultural

Revolution and in a short time transformed itself from a largely impoverished agricultural economy into a very strong industrial power. Much of its population has experienced a thriving economy and far better living conditions. Simply consider the amount of Chinese-made clothes and other products of every kind inundating Western countries' retail stores, online shopping, and manufacturing processes. China is now a rivaling economic titan on the world stage and is representative of the changing global political-economic landscape, globalization, and an inspirational model example to other rising Second and Third World countries today.

I will offer some brief words about the title of this book, which some readers might think peculiar. *Our Emerging World* has two connotations. The first conveys the notion of what is arising in our world, and the second refers to emerging-market countries themselves. Readers will come to notice that these notions go hand in hand because the book explains how emerging market economies will play an increasingly crucial role in how our world is in fact emerging.

My first work focused on how Western thinking has changed over the last five hundred years and where the world stands politically, economically, socioculturally, and environmentally. After I finished that book, I started asking new questions and thinking many things. I eventually realized that many of my thoughts and questions leaned in a certain direction. I felt I had a good grasp on where things stood in the world and why, but I wondered what was coming, where we were headed, and why. These questions spawned this second book. This is knowledge I want to share.

This very up-to-date report's uniqueness is found in the provision of context to modern day political, economic, and societal issues that treated individually do not offer the big picture. The subject at hand is very important, and in one concise volume I provide context not readily available everywhere. This is about my concern to bring forth a better world.

I wrote this treatise also because I wanted to inform the public that the world is about to enter a new chapter in its history; huge political, economic, technological, sociocultural, and environmental changes will occur, and they will affect us and succeeding generations.

Anyone wanting to enter the political arena at any level of government should read my works for they offer a good understanding of the world today and offer indications as to what direction efforts can take in improving the human condition. Much of what we experience individually is occurring in a world setting and circumstances. Understanding this setting and wider world circumstances can help us place our experiences, good and bad, in the current world context and can help us better deal with and cope with what we are exposed to daily. I urge readers to retain facts and extrapolate the context in which they exist. I will have accomplished what I set out to with this piece if readers walk away with a better understanding of our world and where improvements have to be made.

In regard to the negative impacts of human activity on the natural world, I am a contributor to them and as much at fault for that as the next person is. But that does not mean I do not care. My generation inherited many of today's problems. I see myself as evolving with the circumstances we are in, and I foresee that future generations will be even more in tune with such problems and hopefully more inclined to improve matters. I write about such problems because first understanding what we are dealing with is vital for formulating solutions. For the time being, this is my humble contribution.

In 1986, I received a bachelor's degree from McGill University, Montréal, Canada. I studied geography and specialized in a program called Urban Systems. In 1989, I completed a program in management practices at Concordia University, Montréal. I find the field of geography fascinating. It is a field of today and of the future and will become more important because it treats real issues our world is confronted with daily, issues that are becoming ever more complex day by day and require solutions. Think about *National Geographic* magazine and television programs and you will get a good feel of the type of topics involved.

Most people's perception of geography as a field of study involves the identification of hemispheres, countries, capital cities, and location of physical features such as chains of mountains, oceans, and rivers. But geography is much more than that. It is a very intellectually challenging discipline. It is in fact the only academic discipline that takes into account physical and human aspects to explain matters because it is a social as well as a physical science. It is the study of how humans affect the earth and how the earth's physical characteristics affect humans.

No other academic discipline provides such a multidisciplinary and all-encompassing approach to understanding phenomena over space, and it can provide solutions. Geography reminds us that there is a very close relationship between humans and earth and that one affects the other. We often forget this fact in our daily endeavors. A few well-known geographers are England's Prince William, basketball great Michael Jordan, and Immanuel Kant (1724–1804), one of the most influential Western philosophers of all times.

The field of geography has contributed to my life in many positive ways. It has made me understand that human activity affects the earth. It has given me knowledge and context in understanding the world—how the earth works—and approaches to dealing with issues confronting modern society. The field has definitely made me more sensitive to and aware of the problems humanity and the earth face. It has contributed to my realization that humanity's aim cannot constantly be struggle and competition for attaining wealth at the expense of others and the natural world. This realization prompts me to want a better world, one in which all peoples can live in peace in a safe and protected global environment.

People cannot continue to base their decisions concerning life and global politics primarily on how to create prosperity and leave behind the best interests of individuals and the earth. This rationale is partly why I feel qualified to present this book on modern world development. It is founded on my inner desire for a better world, an innocent viewpoint having no ulterior motives and one favorably applauding the survival of all species including our and earth's environment. If we are to ameliorate world problems, we must apply a significantly more concerted global effort and approach to solving them. We still reside in a deeply divided world.

Though my academic background is in geography, I have spent most of my professional career in Montréal's commercial real estate and construction industry in both the private and public sectors and more recently in business investing. I was vice president of business development for an important commercial builder from 2000 to 2005. Prior to that, I dabbled in residential real estate and held posts with commercial real estate companies engaged in the leasing of office and industrial space and market research.

Between 1997 and 2000 and from 2005 to the present, I spent sixteen years employed in regional economic development in Montréal applying my skills and knowledge in a variety of ways, including creating jobs and other positive economic spin-offs by helping attract and settle industrial companies and head offices in the region I represent. I like to think that my efforts contributed positively to my broader community. I feel I am part of the solution. I very much live in reality and am a hopeful thinker.

I enjoy understanding history, people, and the world, and I am concerned about the many social and environmental issues of our time. I particularly like to identify patterns and trends in history and the present and in the world's political and economic development and its repercussions on the natural world and society. I find life to be amazingly beautiful, but I also feel we are living in troubled times. I am not a radical, or an antiglobalist, or an anticapitalist; I consider myself a moderate leftist liberal. I write as part of my legacy and to enlighten those who want to know more about what's going on in the world.

I present many facts in this treatment, but I put them in context. These facts demonstrate that there can be many benefits stemming from globalization but that it can also perpetuate, accentuate, and even cause new social and environmental problems. I choose not to write from the supposition that all our civilization does is bad or wrong. Rather, I write from the perspective that progress can occur differently and not be based solely on the profit motive or market demand and supply.

This book is not intended to mock our historical or contemporary world development or make fun of progress. It is about understanding the shortfalls of the type of progress we've adopted as a civilization and have become accustomed to. We must address these shortfalls and help create new points of view and new approaches to worldwide development to help curtail social and environmental problems. Failing to acknowledge such concerns is like venturing into the forest with our eyes closed.

All around us these days is evidence that world cultures and protection of the natural world are giving way to the profit motive akin to the notion that the new religion is money and economics and that world politics continues to perpetuate it. I am not against money or the accumulation of wealth, but the manner in which we are attaining it is disturbing. There is a lot of what I consider distorted thinking out there, thinking that is bent in favor of profit at the expense of doing the right thing and of commonsense reasoning. I have examples of this sort of reasoning.

First, on the social front, one can think of tied aid—a developed country tries to help a developing country but for its own financial benefit. Think of a developed country providing free tractors to a poor country to help produce crops on the condition that replacement parts for the tractors are purchased from the supplying developed country. I would say that's business, not kindness.

Another example is the discovery of medicines to cure major illnesses such as cancer or diabetes. Sadly, it is claimed, at least for the time being, that such cures cannot be introduced to the public because of the whole business of pharmaceuticals. These cures are withheld from those needing treatment because they are an impediment to the profits of the pharmaceutical companies.

Another example involves higher education. Is it

meant to improve one's chances of obtaining well-paying employment or to contribute to a better world?

A final example is of big business that tracks worldwide megatrends and attempts to turn challenges, chaos, and crises into opportunities to profit, such as world demographic and social changes, technological innovations, and environmental challenges such as climate change and depleting natural resources.

On the environmental front, many companies in advanced countries claim they are in the field of protecting the environment. An example of this is a recycling company I encountered during my career in business. The company recycles only if there's a profit involved. Millions of tons of electronic waste such as computers, other electronic devices, and appliances in developed countries are transported to countries in Latin America and Africa, India, Pakistan, and other Asian countries because legitimate disposal in developed countries is very costly and environmental controls there are very stringent. Also, there is a demand for such waste from companies and organizations in the receiving countries; they generate profits for them. Hence, due to regulatory oversight, ill-enforced laws, loopholes, or outright smuggling by transnational criminal gangs, the waste finds its way to emerging or lesser-developed countries causing damage to the environment and people's health because of very high levels of toxicity coming from plastic and electronic components.

Another example at the environmental level concerns electric and hybrid cars. These are great for the environment in terms of reduction of greenhouse gases, but these cars are currently priced significantly higher than are equivalent gas-powered cars, rendering them financially inaccessible for most. And I question the disposal of the batteries of electric cars. Come to think of it, virtually any product considered good for the environment or human health than the conventional is often priced at a premium.

A final example at the environmental level is that just as a sense of spirituality has been pushed aside in Western society, caring for the natural environment has also been pushed aside, especially when economic times become harsh. Public concern for the status of the natural world has the tendency to accrue when the condition of the economy is in good standing. Shouldn't concern for the natural environment be a constant?

The profit motive often draws our thinking from genuine, not-for-profit measures that could protect the environment or solve pressing social issues. The economic imperative and very strong associated forces are overwhelming; they are leading our world toward more massive growth. My fear is that environmental protection is becoming an industry as any other, an industry highly based on technology to clean nature, create jobs and more innovative technology, and produce environmental protection gear in the name of profit. This same approach is used in questions surrounding social issues. These days, it is less from the heart because it has to make business sense.

Over the last few years, I've acknowledged some

impressive projects and intentions in protection of the environment and of good social causes in communities and other parts of the world. I have taken notice of a few industrial building owners who have adopted geothermal energy as part of their major renovation works. I have seen the occasional office and industrial building built totally on sound environmental principles such as the integration of green or white roofs, the use of gray water, and the reuse of building materials. I have witnessed a politician wanting to develop an industrial park populated only by nonpolluting industrial buildings constructed on sound environmental principles, technologies, and materials.

I have even ascertained that some government leaders in Latin America have successfully attempted to better nourish their populations. I learned from Canadian television newscasts of one high-ranking government leader who wanted to improve life for the aboriginal communities under his jurisdiction, and I have noted another politician in my community who will be adding an ozone treatment phase to the public water supply system to improve potable water quality.

I have even taken notice of former presidents of the United States establishing organizations under their names to contribute and help in all sorts of social causes. I have also witnessed the implementation of recycling programs by municipalities in Canada, and I know of many who give money and time to social causes. I have also concluded that children today are better schooled about environmental issues than past generations have been. There are countless other examples historical and current, but I feel we are still extremely far from deviating from the path of world development that continuously threatens the earth and its peoples and other life forms.

As optimistic as I am, I feel that actions such as those mentioned above stand as well-intentioned symbolic gestures in comparison to the reality and magnitude of the problems we face, but they are steps in the right direction. One Canadian World War II veteran who partook in the 1940 Battle of Dunkirk said something to the effect that "we have developed technology to send humans to the moon, but we still do stupid things."

As tough as I've had to be at times to overcome trying times in my life, I find it difficult to see people suffering, starving, lacking the proper amenities, and being disrespected or physically or mentally harmed. Put yourself in their shoes and tell me how you'd feel! There is still an immense amount of work to be done in relieving human suffering, especially in the Third World. Three-quarters of the world is considered Third World, and we can throw as much money as we want at it to alleviate or attempt to eliminate poverty, but it will always exist until the underlying causal factors are properly dealt with.

About thirty years ago, I would have off-the-cuff conversation with friends and family or initiate discussions on many social and environmental issues confronting us all. Very few really tuned in or cared; many could not relate to the subjects. At that time, the youth especially had little regard for this sort of conversation; they were preoccupied with socializing, having fun, and making money. I concluded that they were correct in regard to their personal ambitions; they needed to go down certain paths if they wanted personal success, but what many failed to grasp was that without a proper natural environment, there would be no future to sustain what they and following generations wanted to achieve.

Without proper human relations and proper treatment of one another, our world is also threatened. One can use the example of the tense US–North Korea nuclear arms crisis of 2017–2018 in which both countries threatened each other with war. Matters fortunately progressed in a positive light in the first half of 2018 as North Korean leader Kim Jong Un suddenly decided to denuclearize North Korea as part of a plan developed with South Korea to denuclearize the Korean peninsula. Kim conveyed his wish to meet with President Trump to hold talks to that effect, and President Trump visited Kim on June 12, 2018, in Singapore. One of the signed agreements concerned complete denuclearization of the Korean peninsula.

However, in late April 2018 and after this historic meeting between the two leaders, there was concern about Kim's seriousness in actually proceeding with denuclearization. It remains to be seen whether Kim will follow through with denuclearization. Many thought it highly unlikely that Kim would give up all his nuclear weaponry. In any event, this important crisis is a reminder of the constant nuclear threat the world is under.

Other examples of the need for proper human relations are the two world wars, the Cold War, the Cuban missile crisis of the 1960s, renewed concerns of a new Cold War, and the escalation of nuclear arms between America and Russia in 2018. Vicious terrorist acts are taking place around the world today, and crazy shootings occur daily. Add to this the plethora of problematic issues and frictions that take place between individuals and groups every day.

# ACKNOWLEDGMENTS

I thank all the teachers who have taught me, especially Joan Glen of the department of geography at Dawson College in Montréal for inspiring me in the study of geography in the 1980s. The professors at McGill and Concordia Universities in Montréal, in particular Professor Sherry Olson of McGill's geography department, inspired me and gave me a good appreciation of what it means to be a geographer.

I also thank my close friend Şukran for her enthusiasm and observations and for encouraging me to write.

I thank my parents and my brother, Filippo, for simply being amazing fixtures in my life.

My thanks go also to other family members and many friends, especially my good friend Tony Fernandes, for the interesting, entertaining, and sometimes challenging conversations we have had over the years.

I extend my warmest appreciation to my colleague and friend Andrea Lane for patiently listening to my ideas and for her encouragement and contributions.

I also extend my warmest gratitude to the rest of the dynamic team at PME MTL West-Island in Montréal, truly an extraordinary organization and group of individuals.

I also thank Montréal's amazing West Island community for having welcomed me with open arms in the mid-1990s.

# INTRODUCTION

The twentieth century was special in a myriad of ways. It was a time of important significance; in the history of humankind, no other century experienced so much change in the human condition.

This hundred-year period is recognized as one of progress, yet it is peppered by many disappointments and contradictions.

The past century gave us great, new technological advances, including aviation, space travel, mass-produced automobiles, computers, television, the Green Revolution, advances in media, the internet, ATMs, and communication devices of all sorts. We also had important discoveries in medicine, including the unraveling of DNA, the contraceptive pill, and cures for smallpox and the Spanish flu.

Socially and politically, the twentieth century will be remembered for favoring equal rights between sexes and races and all civilians, the feminist, black rights, gay and lesbian, and environmental movements, the Cold War and the two world wars, decolonization, and the end of apartheid in South Africa.

Big strides for the betterment of humankind took place in terms of improving and prolonging human life, but that was offset by the development and use of weapons of mass destruction, including chemical and nuclear weapons and intercontinental ballistic missiles.

Numerous wars and revolutions resulted in the deaths of many around the world, often due to differences in political ideology; just think of the Holocaust, the Israeli-Palestinian conflict, and the Vietnam War.

In other cases, authoritarians pushed aside human rights in favor of the state; these included the governments of Cuba, North Korea, Saudi Arabia, Russia, and fascist Italy, Spain, and Argentina, as well as many other countries either considered fascist or sympathetic to fascism in their histories, including Finland, Greece, Chile, Poland, Slovakia, and South Africa.

Along with immense world economic growth, especially in the second half of the century, worrisome and life-threatening impacts on our species and the natural world were identified, and many such issues have not yet been rectified. Globalization certainly gained significantly more traction.

My generation and I have experienced constant change over the last fifty-five years I have been alive; I feel I've lived through two different eras in one lifetime. The first era was not necessarily an innocent time, but it was still influenced by a simpler approach to life, that of the 1960s. The second era, today, is a period I can loosely describe as less innocent.

It is incredible to think how many world and cultural

events you and I have witnessed. Think about all the many religions, cultures, languages, crimes, human and natural disasters, triumphs, tragedies, revolutions and wars, social unrest, and fads and trends we have experienced or learned about. Think about the poverty, injustice, environmental degradation, sadness, illnesses, fear, and social upheavals people the world over have suffered. We have all experienced many changes, but change is normal. However, why has so much changed in such a short time? I wonder where we are headed.

Our world is currently in massive transformation. We are at the cusp of another huge leap and change in Western culture, and most people have no idea this is underway or its amplitude. We've entered a new level and era in world political, economic, cultural, and environmental history, especially because of the intense diffusion of Western culture and technologies causing what is termed as globalization. As my father Salvatore often said in Italian, "Il mondo è un paese," "The world is one country." And he said that well before the terms *globalization and emerging economies* became part of mainstream English. I think he was referring to the growing Americanization of the world, which became more and more apparent during the 1970s and into the 1980s. How true my father's words ring today.

I was involved in family discussions during the 1980s and 1990s held around the huge table my parents would set that was steeped in the southern Italian tradition during the Christmas holidays to accommodate up to twenty people. Around that table, those in my family joked and laughed about all sorts of things, but gone are the Christmas days when we played with toys and board games.

As my brother, cousins, and I grew older, my family started having deeper discussions. In particular, my cousin Fernando, who was six years older than me and one of my favorite role models growing up, my dad, my uncle Gaetano, and I would often discuss religion, the world wars, current events, business, politics, and the economic health of the times. I can recall Uncle Gaetano often wisely stating during such discourses, "Watch out for populous China. That nation will one day be very strong." How true his observation has become and how representative it is of where our world's politics, economy, culture, and environment are headed.

Globalization is the interaction and integration of peoples, companies, and governments of different countries spurred by international trade and business investment. All this is supported by advanced computer technology and the mass media. Globalization impacts cultures, economic development and prosperity, political structures and policy that sustain globalization, dietary and living standards of humans, and the natural environment.

Historically, globalization existed for thousands of years but not to the levels anywhere near what has been evidenced in the last thirty or so years. Some argue that globalization offers poorer countries and their populations lots of opportunities to improve their economic well-being. Opponents on the other hand believe that globalization helps only Western, transnational corporations to the detriment of often less-fortunate countries and their cultures, companies, natural environment, and inhabitants.

In this essay, I want to expand on the world's emerging political, economic, cultural, and environmental changes. Most of us are so bogged down in our work, personal lives, and daily activities—surviving—that we forget about or don't see the big picture. The pre-Trump Western world was already showing signs of a lack of a moral compass and direction, elevated confusion, and insecurity. People strongly consider the Trump presidency to be either positive or negative, and that adds even more domestic and international social confusion and insecurity as individuals are not quite certain of just where things are headed in light of the unconventional and perhaps eccentric ways President Trump views governance and policy formulation and implementation. He appears to offer the world little or no assurance at a time when there are fewer personal and societal boundaries and restrictions.

This discussion is a timely continuation of my first book, *So This Is Where We Stand? How Western Thinking Has Changed over the Last Five Hundred Years* (2016). It is a prerequisite to better comprehending this present book in that it offers a well-rounded understanding of historical and contemporary facts that have shaped and triggered the massive and rising changes taking place in the world right now some of which I treat herein. I offer many observations and conclusions in that essay.

In Chapter 1 of this piece readers will find a few key points from that book that lend themselves nicely to the present report and help expand the topic at hand. Chapter 1 of *Our Emerging World* discusses the Western pattern of economic development since about 1500 and the intensification of that development until and during the Industrial Revolution of the 1800s, as well as new, amplified heights Western development is reaching today. Chapter 2 focuses on emerging and frontier market economies that are poised to contribute to world economic growth and add to and compound much-desired Western economic growth and economic development. Chapter 3 deals with emerging and frontier economies that are modeling their economic development efforts on the advanced part of the world. Of concern here is the increasing threat to global cultural diversity and the rise of a homogenous global culture resembling that of the Western world.

Chapter 4 treats important concerns regarding the natural world and possible solutions. Many countries once considered Third World are rising economically; the impact of this Western-inspired economic growth poses grave concerns for the world. The global environment was already under considerable stress prior to the expected massive contributions emanating from emerging and frontier economies. As such nations rise economically, so will environmental degradation and disaster unless humanity successfully shifts its perspective and adopts a more environmentally sound approach to global economic development allowing the planet to soothe and continue nurturing. This is a tipping point, the basis for ushering in a new way of thinking applied not only to questions surrounding the natural world but societal issues as well, a new thinking I refer to as the new Renaissance. A conclusion ensues.

# CHAPTER 1

## The Western Pattern of Development—A Heightened New Level

### Preindustrial Europe

To provide the reader with supporting facts to this analysis and more important context, presented below is some elaboration on preindustrial Europe. Cipolla (1993, xiii, 137–59, 209–33) explains that from the downfall of the Roman Empire to the beginning of the thirteenth century, Europe was an underdeveloped part of the world that didn't have much to offer and attracted little attention from outsiders in comparison to other civilizations found elsewhere then.

Cipolla wrote that Europe was "a primitive, uninteresting, and underdeveloped corner of the world." China of the T'ang or Sung Dynasties, the Byzantine Empire under the Macedonian Dynasty (867-1056), and the Arab Empire under the Umayyads and the Abbasids were more sophisticated and advanced societies. Descriptions of voyages by Liutprando of Cremona to Constantinople and centuries later by

Marco Polo to China reveal their amazement for the societies they encountered.

Things eventually changed, however. About the year 1000, the European economy accelerated mainly due to international trade. Advancements in skills and technology made European goods more attractive to trading partners. Superior-quality products such as paper, textiles, soap, glass, clocks, and weaponry made from mechanized processes were in great demand by the fifteenth century. Western Europe had economically surpassed many parts of the world by the thirteenth and fourteenth centuries, and that was considered a prelude to the Industrial Revolution of the early 1800s.

At the commencement of 1500, Europe became the most developed and dominant area of the world because of its strong industrial base, and its predominance was not restricted to economics. Europe was to become dominant politically and culturally as well and eventually came to influence world development. This begs the question, what skills and technologies allowed Europe to reach this level of success?

Around 2500 BC, technological innovation virtually came to a halt for the next three thousand years in the Western world. Little progress occurred. By about 1000, however, Europe took off economically, spurred on by expanding trade, manufacturing, and cities. Technological innovation and advancements originated mainly in agriculture. In 1223 and 1246, new revolutionary processes in England's textile industry were so important that some have described it as England's industrial revolution of the thirteenth century. The widespread use and improvement of water mills and windmills created efficiencies in production. The vast improvements made in shipbuilding and improving navigation capabilities offered more economic efficiencies in the transportation of goods.

By 1306, the spinning wheel and spectacles existed. At the outset of the fourteenth century, the first clocks and firearms came into existence. In the 1500s, printed books became more accessible to the public because they cost less to produce due to new print technology, and this further contributed to the spread of knowledge and better education that quickly diffused throughout Europe and beyond.

These few innovations that emerged during the Middle Ages and the Renaissance came about in small steps and after numerous experiments. It was a slow, cumulative process of innovation rather than quick invention, a lot of it rooted in adaptations of ideas developed in other parts of the world. It resulted from the diffusion of technology and skills that spread throughout preindustrial Europe by immigrants, essentially human capital. This eventually set the stage for compounded innovations. No one really knows why Europeans were so taken by mechanization. It took European curiosity and imagination to accomplish innovations, and from at least the thirteenth century, there was a huge interest in the mechanization of productive processes and in problem solving.

The emergence of modern science and the closely

associated Industrial Revolution of the 1800s eventually altered simpler processes and brought forth quicker changes and inventiveness. These resulted in elevated empiricism and mechanization of thought and inventions such as the personal computer and many mechanical and other electrical technologies and inventions we recognize today. And contrary to Greco-Roman times, society moved away from the worldview that humans had to live in harmony with nature.

## A New Level of Global Economic Growth

My first book mentioned in the introduction is all about what they don't tell you in magazines, films, and TV. The media presents world issues and problems but not the underlying dynamics that caused or contributed to the problems. The historical and wider context in which these issues exist is often missing. Worldwide changes are occurring extremely fast and are enveloping the planet due largely to a sharp accentuation in our use of electronic communication technology that prompts higher levels of integration of borderless world trade and financial and economic systems.

The integration of cultures is tied to the past laborious evolution of Western and world development, particularly during the last five hundred years. That period saw enormous, rapid Western expansion in thinking, undertakings, and change that accelerated throughout the 1500s and beyond with increased levels of European colonization. These were the times of the

Renaissance (1350–1620), the Enlightenment (also known as the age of reason, 1715–1789), and the rise of modern science and the Industrial Revolution that began in England (1820–1913).

England's industrialization prompted an intensification of urbanization, the primary setting for the West's economic domination in countries abroad today considered developing or lesser developed. This caused social stratification in industrializing countries, an unequal distribution of wealth in and between nations, and environmental degradation, a by-product of economic growth. Western development was one of constant economic expansion enveloping most parts of the world, one that has largely meant continual rapid societal change and economic growth that caused unequal distribution of wealth globally and of an environmentally destructive kind.

Generally, the Western and predominant worldview prior to 1500 was more natural and spiritual. People lived in small communities and shared with neighbors. Individual needs were less important than were the needs of the community.

For archaic communities, money was important to pay taxes and salaries, but the profit motive was absent from people's mind-sets or simply not allowed. The book continues with a very brief general summary from Capra (1983, 194–96) concerning societal values that became the new norm during the rise of capitalism in the seventeenth and eighteenth centuries.

Although the upcoming paragraph holds true in

spirit to what I discussed in my first book, for purposes of clarity, in parts of the following three pages, I adapt a few additional details from Capra's book mentioned above that are not found in my first book.

The new social values of the seventeenth and eighteenth centuries replaced medieval customs and beliefs that opposed charging interest on loans. The idea was that the prices of goods and services should be fair for all, personal gain and accumulation was discouraged, work was seen as good for the soul and the common good, trade took place for the sufficiency of the group, and true reward would come in the next life. Medieval science was based on reason and religious belief; it was more organic, there was a belief in the sacredness of nature, and the universe was seen as a whole. God, astronomy, ethics, values, soul, feelings and motives, the human spirit, and the five senses were some of the primary elements that helped explain life and the universe.

This was the traditional worldview—a view of the world that all human societies (among them Indigenous Americans, Australian aboriginals, the Chinese Empire, the Persian Empire, the ancient Egyptians, the Indian empire until British rule, the Incas, the Aztecs, the Inuit, the Muslim civilization, and Christian society before the period of Enlightenment) held since the beginning of time.

The modern worldview is the manner people in Europe viewed the world after the seventeenth century period of Enlightenment. This view is rooted in fifth century Greece. Under statesman, general and leader of Athens, Pericles, between 495 and 429 BC Athens reached a supreme period in political dominance, economic growth, intellectualism, the arts, and material prosperity. The focus of the modern worldview is on science; mathematics to explain life, nature and the universe; logic; rationality; critical thinking; and technological and economic progress. It encourages individualism rather than community. At the level of the individual, it causes one to perform and achieve professionally in order to attain material comforts. The modern worldview also espouses autonomy, freedom, success, social status, recognition, and entertainment.

With the rise of modern science and heavy reliance on measurement and quantification (empiricism) came a virtual reversal of that simpler traditional worldview and its attitudes and beliefs. The belief that many of life's problems and inconveniences could be solved with scientific know-how became rampant.

Westerners have noticeably distanced themselves from religious and spiritual influences since the 1500s and have embraced science and capitalism. A massive shift in Western thought that came at the end of the Middle Ages set the stage for the rise of capitalism in the sixteenth and seventeenth centuries and its massive intensification with the coming of the Industrial Revolution.

Western thinking and its approach to life changed dramatically, and that required a capitalist mentality, which was very closely aligned with the religious idea that humans had a calling in life and a moral responsibility to fulfill it. Thus evolved the Protestant work ethic. The accumulation of wealth was generally loathed by Puritans but was seen in a positive light when coupled with industriousness, which was equated with divine destiny. This gave the required impetus and ambition for people to strive and compete, and that allowed for the advancement of capitalism in the sixteenth and seventeenth centuries and the embrace of new values of individualism, property rights, and representative government.

All this led to massive and unprecedented changes in the thinking of Western society, its approach to life, and the way it approached the natural world. Rising capitalism and development entailed a much-needed aggressive human approach toward the natural world, and that prompted the exploitation of all the earth had to offer. This was in part because Western society adopted the idea that earth existed to serve humankind. All earth was subordinated and abused by humankind, and that remains the case today.

In search of more development and economic growth, governments encouraged and provided the necessary political and economic infrastructure that allowed individuals to indulge in this new capitalist mentality. That amplified levels of wealth for corporations and more disposable income for a greater number of individuals.

Today, all industrial economies of the world seek, are heavily addicted to, and are dependent on economic growth. In the West, the growth sought is squeezed from the application of the Keynesian economic trickle-down model of the twentieth century, a national economic system whose success is based on increased corporate spending and investment to create jobs and in turn cause continually higher levels of spending of disposable income by workers to create more national wealth. The thinking is that a portion of this wealth will ultimately reach the poor.

This model is a key reason for the rise of our consumer society. For the system to function properly, continual increased spending by individuals induced by wants and needs is required. This is particularly the case in densely populated urban areas and is stimulated by advertising that sells the public on the attractions of a lifestyle. More demand for everything causes mass production and government-desired economic growth. This approach to economic growth, however, is the main cause of many environmental problems today and an underlying reason for many modern social problems.

This new mind-set bent on work and making a livelihood and corporate profit has caused and is causing humans to become increasingly more scientific and mechanical in their approach to life. It is a less human and a more calculating attitude. The accumulation of wealth has become the new religion, and it is more distanced from the natural world, others, and ourselves. There is now a disconnect between economic growth and human emotional needs. There is also a disconnect between humans and the natural environment. We have become more individualistic, less wholesome, and more alone. There is now the slow disintegration of the patriarchal system, the decline of the fossil fuel era, and cultural changes in terms of morals, values, and beliefs. All three of these phenomena are occurring simultaneously.

Scientific thought and technology has slowly disconnected our thinking from the primary source of human sustenance. For all human history, we have depended directly on Mother Earth for our survival. We need a sense of spirituality for nurturing emotional needs, but today our survival is also dependent on secondary sources, including a slew of technologies. These include chemicals to grow food, satellites that help us communicate and commute, email and SMS texting (which contribute to fewer face-to-face conversations), machines that replace manual labor and do some of our thinking, electricity, money and its pursuit in order to survive, and medical technology of all sorts. Though all this, in particular medicine, doesn't sound so bad, it generally impacts humans by taking our thoughts and actions away from the basics of our sustenance, namely, the earth, spirituality, and closely related, genuine human relations. This is only a sample of how we've thought and lived in the West. A concrete example would be of one asking a young child, where does food come from? They are apt to reply, grocery store shelves! No, it comes from nurturing soil.

By extension, science and the continually intensifying capitalist economy have caused us to lose a certain sense of innocence, and the majority must live in an aggressive, competitive, head-on fashion to survive. This kind of Western thinking is diffusing worldwide.

Gone is the Industrial Revolution that saw a rise

in amazing but simpler forms of technology such as steam-powered locomotives and ships, the machine-based textile industry in England that constituted the first phase of the Industrial Revolution, and the second phase—coal mining, steel, and railroad building.

By 1895, the United States had usurped England as the leading industrial nation in the world. Between 1867 and 1914, Western society experienced the invention of the internal combustion engine, Henry Ford's first mass-produced automobiles, the telephone, the microphone, the light bulb, the bicycle, the typewriter, newsprint, plastics, the first synthetic fibers, artificial silk, the gramophone, wireless telegraphy, pneumatic tires, mechanized public transport, overall increased use of oil and electricity, and initial inroads in the development of the airplane in 1903.

The third phase of the Industrial Revolution lasted from 1890 to the late 1940s and included two world wars. This period witnessed vast, sweeping changes associated with the application of science that caused wide use of electricity in industrial machinery and production and chemicals in the development of such things as dyes, drugs, and industrial commodities.

My first book certainly has much more to offer than this, and it ends by saying that amid all this turmoil and change, there is still hope as private and public groups and individuals everywhere are seeking an innate human need—good for the world. Even the scientific community now acknowledges that the explanation of life and the universe does not have to be empirical and mechanical, that holistic and ecological views are also scientifically sound.

We have entered a new, more advanced part of the Industrial Revolution of the 1800s, that of the information and electronic communication age. We now take off economically once again into a heightened new level of another industrial revolution spearheaded once again by technology and innovation.

In 2018, we are in the advanced stages of the fourth phase of the industrial revolution of the 1800s that commenced around 1950. This era witnessed the early stages of the digital revolution with the eventual change from analog electronics and mechanical devices to digital technology such as semiconductors, personal computers, and the internet in the 1980s and 1990s. These developments have spawned many new forms of information and communications technology, including fax machines, cell phones and other wireless technologies, digital cameras, CDs, digital versatile discs, and high-definition entertainment systems.

The Industrial Revolution of the 1800s served as yet another prelude, a springboard to the coming new type of industrialization witnessed today and envisioned for the future. In 2018, we are witnessing a much more advanced stage of the fourth industrial revolution often referred to as Industry 4.0 with emerging new technologies and inventions in the realms of nanotechnology, the Internet of Things, biotechnology, robotics, artificial intelligence, 3-D printing and television viewing, and driverless cars that can communicate with each other.

Chakravorti (2017, 1) explains that just as the previous industrial revolutions left out many parts of the world from advancement, the current revolution does the same as 4.4 billion global inhabitants have never been online, almost 2 billion have never experienced digital technologies, and 400 million reside outside mobile cellular range. Eighty percent of India has never been online, and that figure is 70 percent for Africans.

The first Industrial Revolution was undeniably the most important of all because subsequent revolutions built upon previous revolutions, and now, since roughly 2005, we have entered a new, higher order referred to as the fifth industrial revolution to unfurl over the next twenty-five years.

This revolution, Industry 5.0, promises to have the highest impact on the world in comparison to the previous four revolutions; it will have the greatest effect on globalization. It will multiply it many times over and at speeds unseen before and envelop the globe. The world will become more interconnected; global networking will join supply chains and the flow of information and cause emerging economies to increasingly partake in the world's manufacturing operations over great distances. It used to be that this type of information flow and exchange of ideas was restricted to rising important urban areas, but now, this shall increasingly take place around a borderless world and with ease.

The Internet of Things, in its infancy in the fourth industrial revolution, will connect new technologies to the point that humans maintain control of processes aided by interconnectivity of electronics and machinery. The Internet of Things is defined as the connection of any device that is electronic or mechanical that basically has an on/off switch and is connected to the internet and other devices from washing machines to coffee percolators and lamps to headphones and airplane engines. Almost anything you can imagine can be connected. We're talking about artificial intelligence and robotics working in conjunction with humans during the manufacturing process. These sorts of scenarios used to be restricted to science fiction movies and television shows but no longer. Business process management software, artificial intelligence, robotics working in tandem with people, and robotic software combined is the foundation of Industry 5.0 (Kospanos 2017). Therefore, one can envision a huge network of connected things including humans. The form it takes is one in which people are connected to people or to devices and devices are connected to devices. As a simple example, you've programmed on the internet that your alarm clock wake you up at 7:00 a.m. and communicate with your bedroom lamp to turn on then. The system then communicates with the sensor in the mechanism controlling your blinds and opens them and tells your coffee percolator to start up. This concept can be applied to manufacturing as well in which humans control the manufacturing processes of widgets via the interconnected web of electronic and mechanical devices that communicate with each other.

What is propelling the fifth industrial revolution?

According to Marsh (2012), first, there will be massive development of many new technologies and new materials, many of which can be used in tandem such as biotechnology and electronics. Second, it will be easier to produce products that cater to the increasing demand for customized and personalized products. Third, there will be a rising importance for products and services for niche industries. Fourth, there will be greater use of global networking resulting in the interplay of supply chains for goods and information conduits for the exchange of ideas. There will also be the creation of business clusters in which companies in different locations can interact with each other and be linked with collaborators around the world.

Fifth, and stemming from this, will be higher levels of participation in the world's manufacturing operations of emerging economies such as those of China and India. Sixth, the manner in which manufacturing takes place and the materials used and produced shall increasingly take into account the protection of the natural world. Finally, there will be a bigger business support system to assist manufacturers in making their products as well as service support systems for manufacturers wanting to engage in out-of-the-box thinking. Businesses big and small that apply one or more of these themes will benefit as the fifth industrial revolution gains more traction over the next ten to twenty years.

The benefits of the first four industrial revolutions were largely geographically restricted to about thirty nations considered advanced today. But after 1990, certain emerging countries led by China became industrially strong enough to become important players on the world stage for the first time in about 150 years. Approximately 150 nations including frontier states will benefit from possible redistribution of world wealth as they participate in the current changes characterizing Industry 5.0 (Marsh 2012).

Presented below are a few examples of how coming changes will affect how we live and work. Some types of human-technological interconnectivity and improvements characterizing industries 4.0 and 5.0 have already existed for upward of twenty years in key manufacturing processes and the military. Only now is this know-how being applied to civilian uses in advanced parts of the world, but over the years it will be used increasingly in emerging markets. Industry 5.0 is inspired by what we see in futuristic science fiction movies and television shows.

**Home Energy Consumption.** Thermostats control more energy than all the other electronic devices used in your home combined. There are devices that learn when you will come home and utilize self-programmed temperature settings, or they respond to a phone call. This will save energy and dollars.

**Home Control Systems.** Homes can now be equipped with systems that can be controlled from tablets so that people can manage their energy use, security systems, lighting, and air-conditioning.

**Office Control Systems.** Office buildings can be equipped with internet technology whereby a building owner or manager can control security, climate, and electrical systems of one or more buildings from anywhere. One can also envision a time when a corporate owner parks her car in the garage of an office building and an automatic signal is given by a sensor that calls an elevator to take her to her office, where she enters with the lights already on as signaled by sensors in the elevator.

**Health Care.** Special sensors can now help doctors and nurses know the status of patients whether they are at home or in the hospital.

**Automobiles.** Key corporations have been attempting to perfect an unmanned automobile, basically robotic, that can sense its surroundings and other cars and navigate without human input. Radar, laser light, GPS, motion sensors, and digital images or videos are utilized in making this endeavor possible.

**Infrastructure.** Electrical power lines, pipelines, and rail tracks can have built-in sensors that transmit data to management teams to determine whether any maintenance is required.

**Airplane Engines.** Special sensors in aircraft engines can now pinpoint developing problems, in part by measuring the temperature of the exhaust and furnish the data to the pilot and maintenance teams on the ground while the airplane is in flight.

In the later stage of the fourth industrial revolution, sophisticated technologies, particularly for electronic communication and transfer of data, are continually being improved, invented, and utilized in the wider society and will become more and more accessible throughout most urban areas in the world.

Western economic development has become ever so expansive causing a heightened new form of Western global colonization and domination. Communication technology and the mass media are helping the West extend its reach in world markets. However, less-developed or developing nations, now referred to as emerging-market economies, are doing the same thing because they too want to develop their economies by applying increased technological know-how and capability in communication; they too want to shower economic gains on their people. Their development is modeled after ours—they've learned from the West how to use expansive thinking and communication technology to their advantage. Thus, Western economies are confronted with increased economic competition from many other parts of the world, and that forces the West to implement more-aggressive, expansive, but protectionist foreign and economic policies.

With political-economic policies, we will increasingly witness the West protecting its interests from outside intervention to control and protect its way of living, well-being, and primary position on the world's political-economic stage. We have seen elevated emphasis of this from the leading nation of the West since the election of President Trump, the United States. One also senses this with Brexit; in 2016, the United Kingdom voted to no longer be part of the European Union. At this time, the United Kingdom will do so by March 2019.

The worry now is that outside cultures are also influencing American and Western society with their own languages, traits, views, and financial clout that contribute to a dilution of Western thinking and culture because outsiders immigrate to Western shores and integrate with the mainstream cultures.

One reason I wrote this book was to convey that the world is becoming ever more spatially interconnected. This is a new level of world integration unseen before, and it is ironic because the spatial diffusion of expansive political-economic thought and actions in the last five hundred years commenced in the West and spread from there to the rest of the world. This diffusion has largely been unidirectional. Make no mistake—many advantages will stem from more borderless spatial interconnectedness, but there will also be a multitude of repercussions. These will include a widening of the economic gap between nations of the world and within nations, especially for the more disadvantaged ones. It also signifies accrued concerns for compounded degradation of the environment as the production, packaging, and consumption of goods increases.

One can envision a rearrangement of the current world

economic and political order to a multipolar type in which there is more than one leading nation in the world. We can also expect elevated homogenization of the world population to resemble that of Western culture and growing resistance and internal struggles in many countries outside the West because of growing pressures from acculturation.

Is Western culture causing changes to the world economy, or is the world economy causing changes to Western society? I say that there is a strong interplay between these questions. I have to conclude, however, that nowadays, economic considerations affect the individual and shape cultures more because we have had the tendency to encourage elements in society that help us prosper as individuals and as countries. As well, we discourage, push aside, or put on hold societal traits that impede people's, nations', and trading blocs' economic advancement and thus alter cultures. An example of this is Western women's wishes, especially during the 1970s, to enter the workforce in large numbers for personal and economic reasons. This contributed to a change in our society and culture and brought forth such societal impacts as the latchkey kid, more disposable income, more individualism, higher divorce rates, and a lessening of the importance placed on the traditional family.

The economy in turn was able to sustain the sociocultural need of the 1970s that caused more demands on the economy and more growth. By extension, situations such as divorce have put demands on the economy because where a couple or family unit resided under one roof, divorce can necessitate two homes for those involved and all the expenses that go along with that for furniture, appliances, a new car, and so on.

Another example is of societies becoming marginalized because their structures, values, and beliefs don't allow them to integrate well with the dominant economic culture such as in the case of indigenous communities. Globalization is prompting economic expansion at the cost of cultural diversity and various societal norms including the declining influence of religion and spirituality.

A final example is the general performance of the economy itself. An economy that isn't growing as fast as we would like it to can restrict upward social mobility for the young in particular and can cause cultural changes; the young might have to become thriftier and perhaps not buy a house, hold back on their other spending, and perhaps delay starting families. Lower rates of marriages and births are characteristics of the emerging Western culture.

The West is still the dominant culture in the world; it affects many global economic aspects and societies. Over the last 500 years and particularly over the last 218 years, economically advanced Western economies, especially that of Britain and above all the United States, have set the world agenda. Who would have imagined other countries could catch up to the West and potentially cause us not to be able to dictate how world development unfurls? Key emerging markets are nonetheless rising and will increasingly affect Western economic power and political policy globally. Western leaders and citizens must be frowning at the thought that countries once considered Third World could become important players on the world political-economic stage.

The key is business. As the last five centuries have shown, aggressive Western colonization was intended for its own economic benefit. It was the West that principally commenced and gained from expansive economic thinking. Now, the whole world is in the game as other countries want to benefit as well from economic activity. The West has set the example for the rest of the world's nations, and they appear not to have a choice but to apply Western approaches to their economic development to grow and have the opportunity to dig themselves out of bad economic circumstances.

Developing nations are striving to improve their economic and social standing. Because of this, I foresee and fear sharply augmented levels of world economic competition and a world economic development in which business is increasingly conducted at any cost. This does not bode well for social and environmental concerns. The West's economic development can generally be described as largely uncontrolled and environmentally destructive. Thus, when the entire world is in the game of economic growth of the same kind as is the case now, we can expect enormous levels of uncontrolled world economic development, progress, and expansion of capitalism. This also means compounded impacts on nature and societies around the world.

Perhaps the world must go through this destructive phase. Does civilization want to greet social, economic, cultural, and environmental catastrophes that deliver decisive societal shocks and awakenings? If the world is lucky enough to overcome such dire circumstances, they may prompt civilization to readjust and become less destructive. We need a more concerted, docile, and nourishing approach to governance and progress to avoid such threatening events.

Modern development and economic growth have been accompanied by destructive technologies and approaches. The questions become, how do we survive without doing business as we know it? How does the world move forward without business? We are in a catch-22 situation—damned if we do and damned if we don't. Business is the driving force of our world economic system. To eliminate or significantly reduce the repercussions, we will have to apply strict management and control. As optimistic as I am, I find it difficult to visualize countries effectively achieving this as each country is fighting for its best interests. A good example is President Trump's stand on putting America's interests first. That meant to him better trade agreements that favored the United States for instance.

The issue of global warming and climate change is another example. There has been much talk in governments and internationally as well as at international forums on the subject, but I have yet to see real progress in curbing global environmental problems. And the leading nation of the world, the United States, eliminated itself from participation in the Paris Climate Accord in 2017. In addition, as of September 2018, domestically, the Trump administration both realized and anticipated changes to US environmental policy. Many actions roll back president Obama-era policy measures that sought to curb climate change and limit environmental pollution and degradation, while other planned actions threatened to limit federal financing for science and the environment.

Our world is divided by territorial boundaries, and it shows in our human relations across borders and in international agreements, laws, and regulations. There is no real unified world governmental or institutional approach to solving important global issues. Political thought and mind-sets reflect state physical territorial boundaries as national governments make decisions that benefit individual countries rather than the global community.

The global economy is certainly becoming increasingly integrated, but our sense of global community is faltering, if not nonexistent. We desperately need to broaden our political perspective from nation to globe. Western nations' politicians, however, play political theater or sometimes camouflage the real issues behind "smoke and mirrors" and focus on micro policy detail in their relentless quest to continually tweak capitalism to maximize national and global economic efficiencies to gain profits.

Emerging and frontier nations will individually or in economic blocs do the same for themselves; they will pull for themselves in an increasingly ferocious competitive global economy. It is the selfish and greedy notion of "to each his own."

I am attempting to illustrate where barriers to solutions to world problems exist. In no way is my intent to demonize any nation, government, or institutional leaders or bodies here, but it's scary as such a situation inhibits the development of solid consensus on global problems let alone proper enforcement of international agreements, laws, and regulations regarding environmental or social ills.

## The World's Biggest Economies

As of August 16, 2018, the nominal gross domestic product of the top ten economies of the world represents more than 67 percent of the world economy. The top twenty economies of the world account for 81 percent. The remaining 172 countries of the world combined account for less than one-fifth of the overall world economy. Below is a list of the ten highest-ranking economies of the world measured by nominal gross domestic product in trillions of dollars.[1]

| | |
|---|---|
| United States | $19.3 |
| China | $12.0 |
| Japan | $4.87 |
| Germany | $3.68 |
| United Kingdom | $2.62 |
| India | $2.61 |
| France | $2.58 |
| Brazil | $2.05 |
| Italy | $1.93 |
| Canada | $1.65 |

---

[1] Source: Prableen Bajpai, 2018.

# CHAPTER 2

## Emerging-Market Economies

To the heightened new level of economic growth taking place in the advanced countries of the world, we must add the rising tide of economic growth emanating from emerging-market economies over the next few decades.

What is an emerging-market economy, and what countries are considered as such? An emerging-market economy is a country that possesses a semblance of a fully developed market economy, such as the United States or Canada, and is on the road to becoming an advanced nation of the world. The limitations with such economies are that they generally have a low level of market efficiency and lack strict standardized accounting principles and securities regulations compared to advanced economies. They do, however, have physical infrastructure such as stock exchanges, banks, and common currencies. These industrialized economies are growing very quickly and demonstrate a very encouraging potential for large growth in their economies, but they do not provide a sufficiently reassuring level of political, monetary, or social stability for outside investors.

Different world organizations don't entirely agree with one another on which countries are considered emerging markets, especially in light of the fact that countries considered as frontier markets, also known as preemerging markets, also exist; these are developing countries with economies that are slower than those of emerging-market countries.

Identified by Jim O'Neill (2001), the top four emerging and developing economies are the BRIC countries—Brazil, Russia, India, and China. South Africa was inducted as a member in 2010, so it is now BRICS. These countries have not formed an official economic bloc, but there are indications that they may want to form an alliance to give them more geopolitical clout.

Evidence suggests that these nations are amassing more economic power as a united front and are influencing the world economic order by taking economic power from advanced G-6 states—the US, Japan, UK, Germany, France, and Italy—and are redirecting it to the developing world. Wilson and Purushotham (2003) predict that BRIC countries together will surpass the G-6 economies by 2039. It is the first time in history that such a situation presents a scenario in which the world has the potential for a multipolar power global political system rather than a unilateral one, and that could play havoc with the global balance of power.

Could this be the start of the decline of the Western

world? For the time being, America and the rest of the Western Bloc are still calling the shots on the world stage. An important fact is that one or more of the BRICS nations can be replaced at any time by up-and-coming nations who economically outperform nations currently forming BRICS.

According to Wilson and Stupnytska (2007), the next eleven emerging economies are Bangladesh, Egypt, Indonesia, Iran, Mexico, Nigeria, Pakistan, Philippines, South Korea, Turkey, and Vietnam. Of these, *Bloomberg News* (2012) says the four most prominent are Mexico, Indonesia, South Korea, and Turkey, given the acronym MIST nations.

The FTSE Group (2016) list of twenty-seven countries considered as frontier markets: Bahrain, Bangladesh, Botswana, Bulgaria, Côte d'Ivoire, Croatia, Cyprus, Estonia, Ghana, Jordan, Kenya, Latvia, Lithuania, Macedonia, Malta, Mauritius, Morocco, Nigeria, Oman, Palestine, Romania, Serbia, Slovakia, Slovenia, Sri Lanka, Tunisia, and Vietnam.

The Industrial Revolution of the 1800s occurred because of many forces coming together at an opportune time in world history and unleashing unprecedented levels of upheaval and change in ideas, values, beliefs, social structures, and economic growth and personal wealth of the likes we may never witness again. This is radical change to the point that the face of reality was altered and brought life to what we know it as today.

Since the powerful economic slowdown of 2008, now in 2017, it appears that economic growth has petered out and the new economic norm of slower growth has taken hold of the West. Today, only 2 percent annual growth in GDP is considered good for a developed country. The economic crisis of 2008 also appears to have negatively affected the BRICS countries. According to the *Economist* (2013), the growth of BRICS economies beginning in the late 1990s quite impressively outpaced that of the United States by 3.3 percent per annum. It is expected that emerging economies will continue to slowly grow in economic importance, but it appears their biggest gains have already been made, as growth rates in these countries have decreased, causing them to have less clout throughout the world.

Nonetheless, the world economy has grown since 1990, and this trend will continue as globalization takes place. The important trend to underline is that countries considered developing or less developed are on the rise economically albeit at a slower pace, but this will translate into important changes in different world cultures and their natural environments. Emerging nations are the wild card in how world politics and economic growth will unfold in the near future. They may rival the advanced nations of the world, but their economic growth, whether faster or slower, will contribute to global economic growth.

In an extensive report, economists Hawksworth, Audino, and Clarry (2017) stated that emerging markets would continue to be the growth engine of the world economy. They project that the world economy could more than double in size by 2050. By 2030, it is projected that the top-ten countries of the world will be in order of importance China, United States, India, Japan, Indonesia, Russia, Germany, Brazil, Mexico, and the United Kingdom. The top-ten world economies of 2050 will probably be in order of importance China, India, United States, Indonesia, Brazil, Russia, Mexico, Japan, Germany, and the United Kingdom.

The emerging-seven economy (E-7)[2] is projected to overtake the G-7[3] by around 2030. This means there will be an important shift in global economic power in which the G-7's share of world gross domestic product will fall to 20 percent from 31 percent today and that of the E-7 will rise from 37 percent today to 50 percent. This also means more pressure on the world environmental system emanating from these rising powers because of continued and rising $CO_2$ emissions, demand for land for housing, more manufacturing, more transport of goods, more use of cars and airplanes, and more demand for electricity and heating.

A primary reason for the emergence of these new economies is that advanced nation economies are performing at lower levels since the 1990s in comparison to highly performing economies of the developing world. The worldwide financial crisis of 2008/09 contributed to the already existent downward economic trend of advanced economies. This means that emerging

---

[2] E-7: the emerging-market economies of Brazil, China, India, Indonesia, Mexico, Russia, and Turkey.

[3] G-7: the advanced economies of Canada, France, Germany, Italy, Japan, the United Kingdom, and the United States.

economies are catching up with the economies of the developed world and are forecast to outperform many of them by 2030. This will have an impact on the present worldwide balance of economic power.

The implications of the new economic order are twofold: first, as household revenues and populations increase, so will the demand for Western goods and services from these markets, especially from young consumers. This demand will increasingly originate from highly populated and urbanized emerging economies. Second, there will be more investment originating from emerging nations destined toward the developed world, but investment by the developed world in emerging countries will also occur and cause the emerging economies to flourish further.

An Ernst & Young report (2013, 2–9) states that the world witnessed a first expansion of the middle class in Europe and the United States in the nineteenth century created by the Industrial Revolution. A second expansion in the growth of the middle class occurred after World War II in Europe and North America. The third expansion of this class is taking place today in emerging economies. Estimates call for an expansion of the middle class almost exclusively in the emerging world of three billion people over the next twenty years. By 2030, it is projected that two-thirds (66 percent) of the global middle class will be in the Asia-Pacific region with the North American middle class representing 7 percent, Europe 14 percent, Central and South America

6 percent, the Middle East and North Africa 5 percent, and sub-Saharan Africa 2 percent.

Also by 2030, considerable numbers of people globally will no longer live in poverty, and that will completely change the balance of geopolitical power; international trade patterns will be unrecognizable. Over the next twenty years, big populations and substantial economic growth will cause China and India to become the new powerhouses of middle-class mass consumerism, as well as additional contributions made by other emerging economies particularly those of Mexico and Brazil.

In terms of the global distribution of wealth, the gap in per capita income between developed and emerging economies has been decreased, but throughout the emerging markets, urban households enjoy significantly higher incomes than do those in rural areas. It is thought that this trend will continue to 2030, but a more equitable distribution of wealth between countries is expected. Right now, we are still very far from an equitable distribution of world wealth.

## Disruptive Global Economic Forces

According to Dobbs, Manyika, and Woetzel (2015), four strong and disruptive global forces are happening simultaneously; they are breaking all the trends and causing great change to the global economy. They state that urbanization, accelerated technological change, an aging world population, and greater global connectivity are the causes. They estimate that in comparison to the Industrial Revolution of the late eighteenth and early nineteenth centuries, the dramatic changes we are beginning to witness are occurring ten times faster and at three hundred times the scale and thus having about three thousand times the impact. The changes are gaining strength as they are multiplying by interacting, blending with each other, and feeding upon one another, thus producing monumental change.

Just as urban areas were the principal settings that allowed for control of territories outside the West through colonialism and for the spread of capitalism, urban areas are the setting of the global economic changes taking place today. Economic activity and vitality are shifting to emerging markets such as China and to urban areas in those countries. Emerging-market economies are experiencing industrial and urban revolutions while causing shifts in economic activity from North America and Europe to eastern and southern parts of the world at incredible speed.

It is expected that by 2025, half the world's large corporations with revenues of $1 billion or more will be headquartered in the cities of emerging-market countries such as Mumbai, Dubai, and Shanghai and in cities we've never heard of before such as Hsinchu in northern Taiwan and Tianjin, a city about 120 kilometers southeast of Beijing. This will be because of increasing population levels in these cities and growth in local gross domestic product.

Urbanization is a true megatrend. McKinsey Global Institute (2012) says that a wave of urbanization is propelling growth in emerging economies. The millions of people relocating to cities the world over are increasing their incomes. It is expected that by 2025, about six hundred million people will enter around 440 cities in emerging markets and join the consuming class. They are expected to generate close to half the global gross domestic product growth between 2010 and 2025.

Incomes in developing economies are rising faster and on a bigger scale than at any other time in history. This entails more construction of buildings and urban infrastructure as well as a stronger demand for the world's natural resources and capital.

The second factor causing global economic transformation is the technological change occurring at an exponential rate never witnessed before. Changes in technology and innovation have always been identified as a big force in challenging and changing the status quo. The magnitude and speed of this change and its economic impact and omnipresence in our lives are compounded now more than ever and at a very high rate. For instance, it took over fifty years after the invention of the telephone before half the dwellings in America had telephones, and it took thirty-eight years for radio to attract an audience of fifty million. In comparison, Facebook had six million subscribers in its first year, and that number was multiplied a hundred times over in the next five years. It took the smartphone less than ten years to be used by half the American population.

A third factor that contributes to global economic change is the world's aging population. Developed countries have been experiencing declining birth rates and an aging population; these trends have been confirmed in places such as China, Thailand, and countries in Latin America. Two areas of significance for the global economy that will be affected are first the creation of a smaller global workforce. This means that more focus will be placed on productivity for creating economic growth and uncertainty as to overall global economic performance. Second, taking care of a graying world population will put great pressure on government budgets and finances.

The final disruptive force affecting the global economy is higher levels of global connectivity by the movement of capital, people, and information. Modern globalization used to be characterized by simpler linear connections between key markets in Europe and North America, but this is no longer true. Aided by technology, the interconnectivity of markets is now vaster as a new level of globalization has occurred in which we are no longer talking about linear connectivity but a web of connectivity now including Asia and Africa and other emerging markets. This has meant more opportunities for higher levels of global trade and finance, but it also means more global economic insecurities because negative economic, political, social, and environmental events and circumstances that happen in a given part of the world can harm the economic growth and stability of other markets intertwined in the web.

Another disruptive force that will cause change in the global economy is the expected formation of new, huge, economic blocs that will spring up in different parts of the globe to elevate their level of political and economic clout against competing nations and other such economic blocs.

# CHAPTER 3

## One World, One Culture

Cultures can remain intact for long periods because they are preserved and protected by religious beliefs or political rules. Some cultures are resistant to change and impede new ideas or technologies from influencing them while other cultures welcome change and open themselves to outside influences.

With Western globalization, cultural impacts are being felt in most parts of the world including in emerging, frontier, and less-developed markets. Higher levels of economic integration with the West mean global cultures are opening their doors to Western morals, values, beliefs, lifestyles, and technologies. For more-conservative cultures, this means changing their ways of living and what they believe. This will increase friction and upheaval in populations that do not want to resemble the West.

But other world societies welcome Western culture with open arms, and China is a prime example of this. Particularly since the 1980s, China has been using

Western technology of all sorts as well as adopting a Western lifestyle. This is evidenced by the use of Western clothing, cell phones, viewing American television shows, and going to American fast-food outlets. Chinese students are required to learn English at a young age. It is becoming very apparent that cultures are changing everywhere in the world even if certain countries want to resist change; this is occurring because of increasing integration with the Western world via international commerce, the internet, and the mass media.

What is the West communicating culturally to the rest of the world? All religions of the world have in their own ways contributed to civilization, and they will continue to do so just as Christianity has and will continue to do. I want to, however, focus on Christianity at this moment because it has been a widely spread faith and certainly the predominant religion of the West. It is ingrained in Western society and the thinking and messages the West has spread around the world.

In a recent voyage to Italy and in particular Rome, the Vatican, and Florence, I was amazed to see how influential Christianity once was as many parts of the Bible are brought to life in urban landscapes represented by unbelievable biblical stories found in architecture such as churches and monuments and landscapes, wonderful statues, artifacts, and paintings. Stansberry (2007) writes that the Bible spawned a lot of the language, literature, and the fine arts we enjoy today. Christianity has been a leading religion in the world, and its doctrine and philosophy caused positive changes in the world. It was the foundation that held up Western culture and provided enormous positive structure and influence for its population. Whatever negatives we may associate with it are outweighed by its overall benefits for humankind; it simply made us better. Western Christian values influenced governments to provide people education, liberty, rights, and justice. It also caused the beginnings of science because the fathers of modern science held deeply religious beliefs.

Especially over the last five hundred years, Christianity has been a huge contributor to the improvement of living standards in the West, and it plays an important role in the lives of millions around the world today by offering comfort, strength, inspiration, hope, morals, values, identity, and structure for living. It also provides a stage for the different celebrations of life—baptisms, first communions, confirmations, masses, marriages, and funerals.

On a wider scale, as Western society has slowly moved away from Judeo-Christian morals, values, and beliefs and has increasingly embraced the scientific world, it has created a spiritual vacuum in our culture. Because of this, many societal problems have arisen. A clash has developed between the more humble approaches to life that Christianity preaches and the aggressive, competitive, money-domineering capitalist society we are.

We acknowledge the effects of this at the individual level—general moral decay represented by violent crime, divorce and the decline of the nuclear family, drug abuse, fraud, corruption, materialism, individualism, and self-indulgence. Mediocrity is accepted over the pursuit of excellence. Christianity was the foundation that held up Western culture and provided enormous positive influence for its populations. It provided direction for societies and individuals alike. With such an important cultural influence largely pushed aside, as evidenced by the division between church and state, for example, to whom or what do we look for direction and inspiration? It is often said that no individual and no society can regain composure without some sense of the spiritual.

The West is certainly no longer exporting Judeo-Christian religion and spirituality and their related positive societal attributes described above that provide a degree of posture and composure for societies to other corners of the earth in the traditional missionary sense. It is, however, exporting its current lifestyle, technology, problems, and hopes. The West has sold its modern way of living around the world, and there have been takers. Other cultures want what the West has to offer, and they are going after it. Something developing nations underestimate or do not take into account is the negative aspects associated with Western culture that eventually become assimilated in their own societies. Eckersley (2012) argues that over the last twenty years, Westerners are somewhat happier than in the past but appear to be more pessimistic, especially when it comes to uncertainties revolving around the economy and the natural environment. They are more anxious, greedier, and more selfish. They live under the aura of consumption and competition and express little empathy. They are less community oriented, there is a lot of stress on their families, and they are exposed to drugs, crime, and violence. They enjoy freedom and material wealth but have trouble appreciating what they possess; they have an insatiable desire for more of everything.

Such cultural traits have led individuals to strive, compete, perform, and become more selfish—thus the rise of individualism, which contributes to our personal, self-styled image no longer shaped by communal cultural traditions, values, and beliefs. This is true for the wealthiest in Western society as well as for those in the lower echelons of the economic strata. The West is introducing this cultural crisis to other populations of the world.

An important part of the Western cultural crisis we are propagating at amplified levels around the world is what the Cree call *wétiko*, a diabolically wicked person or spirit that terrorizes others and that unfortunately for the last two thousand years has in large part been part of world history. Indigenous peoples believe wétiko is an invisible disease in the human psyche, soul, and spirit at the level of the individual, between individuals, and collectively on a worldwide scale. Wétiko disease arose when civilization began. Forbes (2008) describes this disease as the greatest epidemic sickness known to humankind. It stems from the innermost depths of the human psyche and represents a great lack of security for our individual and perhaps collective survival.

This has reached an exaggerated level as we strive for much more than necessary. We continue to strive for all that makes us feel secure. Forbes stated that modern civilization suffers from an overly one-sided dominance of the rational, intellectual mind, a one-sidedness that is the culprit disconnecting individuals in society and society collectively from nature, empathy, and ourselves. Because of this disconnect, wétiko disturbs the peace of humanity and the natural world, a sickness that can cause aggression and is capable of bringing forth violence for humanity. According to Forbes, "The wétiko virus is the root cause of the inhumanity in human nature, or shall we say, our seemingly inhuman nature."

John McMurty (1999) refers to it as the greatest sickness that pervades our modern capitalist society as though it were a cancer and that we've entered a cancerous phase of capitalism. Forbes says that wétiko is like cannibalism for those under its spell because it consumes others' lives for their own purposes or profit without returning anything. Many don't think twice about wétiko because they have no idea of its existence. This collective insanity is so pervasive that it seems normal. It manifests itself at the collective level by our extremely consumer-oriented society, a culture that continuously creates wants and needs to insatiable degrees to fill the spiritual void without regard for the environment or societal factors. This is designed and supported by governments and corporations, but this imbalance of the mind could cause the demise of humankind.

In this time of societal bewilderment and confusion, Westerners generally lack direction. We are collectively having difficulty finding what to believe in next. We have lost a collective peace of mind. We are continually evolving and searching for a new identity and a raison d'être. When we peel away at individual anxiety, we discover that it does not have its roots in uncertainties associated with environmental problems, economics, the threat of war, or political inconsistencies. In this cultural spiritual vacuum and a time of strong belief in scientific truth, individuals are anxious because they do not know what roles to pursue, what principles to adopt, and what direction to take.

From birth, we are thrown into the abyss, and we all strive to turn our chaotic lives into ordered lives. Order means survival, and a strong sense of the spiritual contributed to the order we seek. Religion and spirituality meant customs, rituals, and norms. Rules such as the Ten Commandments provided people guidance and personal fulfillment. They were passed down from one generation to the next, but their downplay or absence has left the newest generations at a loss. Something innate in humans calls for order so we can survive. We may not like rules, but we constantly seek and apply them to give order, structure, and meaning to our lives.

As we Westerners slowly shed the religious and spiritual influences of the past, we seek new rules, customs, norms, and rituals to give our lives meaning and make them pleasant in a world built on machinelike science and the profit motive. However, we have yet to clearly define these new rules, customs, norms, and rituals, so we appear to be living bewildered, powerless, and empty lives of despair, confusion, and insecurity. We are alone and in limbo. We don't know what we want and feel. All of this causes anxiety. Thus, in today's world, May (1981, 40) says that a person's individual anxiety can be described as a basic reaction to a perceived threat to the survival of the individual or to a value or set of values that the individual holds important to his or her existence.

Perhaps a new worldview will arise from this confusion, insecurity, and transformation, but that is not in focus and is still very far off. Reaching clarity on this matter is an arduous endeavor most are not even aware is taking place. This is part of the Western cultural crisis spreading around the world.

On the way to attaining clarity, fortunately, I sense somehow that the newest generations seek the truth and good that can be foundational factors in the shaping of a new worldview. In tune with this argument, Andrea Lane, interviewed in January 2018, expresses with much hope,

> In the event of globalization we are being exposed to other traditions, religions and points of view that are causing us to reflect on our own morals, values, and beliefs and reevaluate if they still hold true. Usually in a time of change there are a few steps backward, reassessment before we move forward. I choose to believe that we are living in a time of reassessment, purging the ideas that are no longer serving us and reembracing the true spirit in which our religions, traditions and beliefs were created—the spirit of unconditional love, acceptance, well-being for all.

The Western cultural crisis, which includes wétiko and the hopeful possibilities presented in the above paragraphs, are what the West is globalizing. With the current pattern and methods of world economic development sustained, global cultural diversity is threatened.

An element closely associated with globalization is the homogenization of cultures. The world's cultural diversity is perceived in a very positive light, but it is threatened by globalization. The market segment highly targeted by Western transnational corporations is the young. It is easier to lure them away from their cultural traditions because they have not yet been highly immersed in them. Such pressures stemming from outside sources will lead to the dilution or total abandonment of indigenous traditional values and beliefs causing such societies around the world to slowly disappear and significantly reduce global cultural diversity. That will give rise to one huge, homogenized Western culture worldwide. If in support of globalization, indigenous peoples often want protection and perpetuation of their cultures, their governments should support that. They wish for economic development while holding onto their cultures, but that might be a passport to the slow erosion of non-Western cultures because pressures from the dominant world culture can eventually overtake the less-potent ones.

Over the horizon, therefore, is expected the development of one global culture resembling the current dominant Western one that promises those it influences freedom, opportunity, and prosperity but accompanied by obscure realities, including its anemic spiritual influence, cultural crisis, search for itself, and transformation—problems of all sorts but strangely enough but happily, hope.

# CHAPTER 4

## Concerns for the Natural World and Possible Solutions

### The Natural World

When considering the world's natural environment in correlation with higher levels of global economic development due to rising globalization, we cannot overlook the compound effects on nature bound to take place if largely uncontrolled development continues to unfold.

I can write about an array of specific environmental problems stemming from world economic development, including deforestation, soil erosion, air, noise, and water pollution, ozone depletion, depletion of nonrenewable resources, acid rain, endangered species of flora and fauna, radioactive waste, and many others. All environmental problems are important and have an enormous impact, but I will not discuss them in that light. I will put all these issues into context in upcoming paragraphs.

Many believe that environmental problems are due

simply to climate change. That's all we hear on the news or read about when it comes to the environment. We really can't blame those who are unaware as we walk around in most cities and rural areas of Europe, North America, and other parts of the advanced world and all appears to be just fine. The environmental problems, however, are lurking where one doesn't see—behind the production, packaging, and consumption of products. What resource requirements and environmental damage is involved with constructing a skyscraper, producing food, or transporting widgets around the world? What the unaware often do not comprehend is that climate change is but one problem along with many others. One thing is certain—many environmental problems stem from our cultural attitudes toward the environment and human activities and approach to economic development and growth. This excludes environmental damage or change caused by natural phenomena.

Having observed the larger picture of the many social and environmental ills of our time, I cannot underestimate the role that modern science has played. Unquestionably, modern science has allowed vast changes for the better and has improved living standards particularly in the West in immeasurable ways. It's a wonderful, comforting feeling to know that we can live in the coziness of our homes and enjoy all sorts of amenities. It is equally soothing to know that virtually anything we want is available wherever and whenever we want it. It takes a lot of resources to live in this manner, and it took much scientific knowledge and breakthroughs to help us reach this point. But it seems that science as applied today often interrupts natural processes, particularly in regard to the natural world— nature appears not to be digesting science very well.

Science and related aspects tied to economic growth and consumerism appear to go against many of the laws of nature and contribute to social ills. Consider the adoption of modern medicines that has decreased the death rate but thus boost global overpopulation. Think about antibiotics that have promoted the evolution of bacteria that current biotechnology cannot combat. Plastics take an inexplicable amount of time to biodegrade, and cell phones raise questions about the impact of microwaves on human health.

Science has also caused the invention or improvement of many technologies involved in warfare, including nuclear and chemical weaponry. Sonar is a huge contributor to overfishing of our seas. The ability to fly by plane contributes to the quick spread of infectious and possibly pandemic diseases. And chemical technology used in agriculture threatens soil, water, aquatic life, and even public health.

We can explain and put into context global stresses on the natural world and their repercussions on humanity by discussing four massive factors—the Anthropocene epoch, inadvertent global climatic change, world population growth, and rising levels of urbanization.

# The Anthropocene Epoch

The Anthropocene is a proposed epoch dating from the start of significant anthropogenic impact on the earth's geology and ecosystems. As of August 2016, neither the International Commission on Stratigraphy (ICS) nor the International Union of Geological Sciences has yet officially approved the term as a delineation of a geological time. But the British-led Working Group on the Anthropocene (WGA), which started work in 2009 and is a subcommission of the ICS, voted to formally designate the epoch Anthropocene and presented the recommendation to the International Geological Congress held in Cape Town, South Africa, on August 29, 2016.

The International Chronostratigraphic Chart shows scientifically verified changes to the earth's upper crust and dates when a global event happened or a change in time interval occurred, such as an era or epoch over the four-and-a-half-billion-year history of the planet. The ICS is responsible for making amendments to the chart and is very strict about altering the geological time scale as it considers many factors when considering a change in time interval. Although the WGA has recommended to the ICS that it delineate and declare the new Anthropocene epoch on the chart, the ICS must assess and accept the recommendation, and that could take two years.

The word *Anthropocene* did not exist twenty years ago, but it is now imbedded in the scientific community and radiating outward. It will eventually become a commonly used term just as *climate change* is now. Anthropocene refers to a new epoch, one in which humanity is the central actor in altering the earth's environmental systems by its activities. The new epoch can also be referred to as the age of humans.

The previous epoch is the Holocene; it began 11,700 years ago when glaciers began to retreat and the world attained a stable, warmer climate allowing human civilization to develop. Scientists have recently declared that we have left the Holocene and are in the Anthropocene epoch; the earth has left its natural geological epoch of the last half-million years and entered one human activity profoundly impacts. The magnitude of activity and change involved is unprecedented and considered unsustainable. It could cause the natural environment to respond in unpredictable and dangerous ways.

The Anthropocene epoch emerged with the rise and intensification of capitalism, colonialism, the Industrial Revolution, and the use of fossil fuels. The scientific community generally agrees that this epoch began in 1950, a time when the compound effects of eighteenth-century industrialization became extremely noticeable across various socioeconomic parameters; it is called the great acceleration. Exponential levels of growth were reached in 1950 in terms of world real gross domestic product, world population growth, urban population growth, the use of water, energy, and agricultural fertilizer, foreign direct investment, transportation, international tourism, the production of paper, and telecommunications (Angus 2015). These parameters peaked sharply in 1950; the last fifty years of the twentieth century experienced the most rapid and greatest impacts in human history in terms of change for the environment due to human activities.

Angus (2015) makes reference to the existence of defining points in the earth's geologic time line that mark the change of eons, eras, periods, epochs, and ages. The geologic time line encompassing the four-and-a-half-billion-year history of the earth consists of four eras—Precambrian time, the Paleozoic era, the Mesozoic era, and the Cenozoic era. Geologists divide the earth's history into spans marked by various events and conditions. We are currently living in the Quaternary period in the Cenozoic era, which dates back 65 million years. The Quaternary is thus divided into two epochs—the Pleistocene, which commenced 2.58 million years ago, and the Holocene, which began 11,700 years ago.

Each interval of change—eons, eras, periods, epochs, and ages—is reflected in a clearly defined status of the earth and life forms and is recorded in the earth's crust. For example, the last glacial retreat marks the beginning of the Holocene epoch or mass extinction marked the end of the Mesozoic era when all dinosaurs and many other animals ceased to exist. The Cenozoic era we live in today is marked by the rise of mammals that survived the Mesozoic that grew and inhabited the earth, and that includes humans.

Geologists utilize physical proof known as

stratigraphic markers in the earth's crust to create a geologic time line of changes in eons, eras, periods, epochs, and ages and to prove that there have been major changes to the environment between one period and another. Proof is found in rock, sediment, ice, and fossils, but proof is also found in other ways.

The scientific community has debated what stratigraphic markers should be used to prove that the earth has passed from the Holocene to the Anthropocene epoch. Scientists have decided that the principal stratigraphic markers are radioactive plutonium fallout left in the atmosphere after nuclear bomb testing at the start of the Cold War beginning with the 1945 New Mexico tests, disposable plastics, and exponential global population growth (Castree 2016). Other potential markers are soot from nuclear power stations, human-engineered concrete, aluminum particles, and bones from domesticated chickens as well as the rise of carbon dioxide emissions, rises in the sea level, the global mass extinction of flora and fauna, the rise of nitrogen and phosphorous in soils, deforestation, and urban development (Carrington 2016). The combustion of coal must also be added as associated soot became evident in the geological strata around the world in about 1950.

Entry to the new Anthropocene epoch can best be described by the following citation from John Bellamy Foster (Angus 2015).

In the period after 1945 the world entered a new stage of planetary crisis in which human economic activities began to affect in entirely new ways the basic conditions of life on earth. This new ecological stage was connected to the rise, earlier in the century, of monopoly capitalism, an economy dominated by large firms, and to the accompanying transformations in the relation between science and industry. Synthetic products that were not biodegradable—that could not be broken down by natural cycles— became basic elements of industrial output. Moreover, as the world economy continued to grow, the opening up as never before the possibility of planet-wide ecological disaster. Today few can doubt that the system has crossed critical thresholds of ecological sustainability, raising questions about the vulnerability of the entire planet.

It appears humankind has been able to exercise some control over nature and is now the principal driving factor behind the changes caused to the earth's natural environment. There is serious concern over our level of global societal preparedness to contend with environmental problems alone in the Anthropocene epoch as the new epoch surprises humanity with scenarios, circumstances, and challenges that too frequently surpass our ability to comprehend what can occur, is occurring, and has occurred. It is a conundrum that shall test democracy.

The impact of human activity in the Anthropocene epoch is worldwide and irreversible commencing with climate change and leading to the loss of biodiversity and environmental degradation. Humans are affecting the environmental system that supports life. It is akin to astronauts fiddling with their spacecraft's life-support systems in outer space.

As this treatise and my first book attempt to do, the literature says that there is a need to better understand the underlying societal causes of environmentally destructive human activity and capitalism in the post–World War II era.

## Inadvertent Global Climatic Change

Pidwirny (2006) provides a very good account of earth's climate history. It is clear from his description that the earth experienced warmer and colder periods throughout its history. He says that climatologists have found that during most of earth's history, global temperatures were probably 8–15 degrees Celsius warmer (46.4–59.0 degrees Fahrenheit) than today. In the last billion years, warmer climatic conditions were interrupted by numerous glacial periods up to two million years before the present.

The period 2,000,000 to 14,000 before the present is known as the Pleistocene epoch or Ice Age during which glacial ice sheets covered most of North America, Europe, and Asia for long periods. The Ice Age had periods when glacial ice retreated because of warmer temperatures and advanced because of colder temperatures. During the coldest periods of the Ice Age, it is estimated that mean global temperatures were probably about 4–5 degrees Celsius (39.2–41.0 degrees Fahrenheit) colder than today.

We are presently in the most recent glacial retreat. This is called the Holocene epoch, a warmer period that began some fourteen thousand years ago (12,000 BC). By 5000 to 3000 BC, mean global temperatures reached their warmest, 1–2 degrees Celsius (33.8–35.6 degrees Fahrenheit) warmer than today, and that period is known as the Climatic Optimum. During that time, many great ancient civilizations rose and flourished.

Between 3000 and 2000 BC, the earth experienced a cooling trend causing a significant drop in sea levels that brought to the surface many islands such as the Bahamas and many coastal areas. Colder temperatures from 1500 to 750 BC were the cause of ice collecting in continental and alpine glaciers.

During the time of the Roman Empire (150 BC–AD 300), cooling commenced and lasted until approximately 900. At its peak, the cold was so intense that it froze the Nile River (in 829) and the Black Sea (in 800–01).

What is called the Little Climatic Optimum occurred between AD 900 and 1200. It was the warmest period since the Climatic Optimum, and it allowed the Vikings to settle in Greenland and Iceland.

Between 1550 and 1850, global temperatures were at their coldest since the start of the Holocene. Scientists have coined this time period as the Little Ice Age, and it caused average annual temperatures in the northern hemisphere to reach approximately 1.0 degree Celsius (33.8 degrees Fahrenheit) lower than today.

From 1580 to 1600, the Western United States experienced one of its longest and most severe droughts in the last five hundred years. From 1753 to 1759, cold temperatures in Iceland caused a quarter of the population to die from failures in agriculture and resultant famine.

I find it appropriate to add the following paragraph to Pidwirny's description. The year 1816 is widely known as the Year without a Summer, or the Poverty Year. North America, Europe, and Asia were affected by cold temperatures during the summer causing vast failure in agriculture leading to major food shortages and famines. Earth had already been experiencing cooling in the past century that started in the fourteenth century with the Little Ice Age. This period had caused many problems in the cultivation of foodstuffs in Europe. Almost at the end of the Little Ice Age, temperatures declined further by 1816 because of the major volcanic eruption of Mount Tambora on the Indonesian island of Sumbawa in April 1815. That caused a volcanic winter, and according to Stothers (1984), it decreased global temperature a further 0.4–0.7 degrees Celsius (32.7–33.2 degrees Fahrenheit).

The various literature on the subject referred to describes different parts of the world—from Canada to China—as being affected in different ways depending on location. The year 1816 can sweepingly be described as a time of agricultural disaster, famine, food riots, frost and abnormal rainfalls and flooding, epidemics—typhus and cholera in particular—strange weather phenomena such as a June snowfall of 30 centimeters (11.8 inches) in Québec, Canada, and death.

In the 1930s and 1950s, the central United States found itself in conditions of extreme drought.

From 1850 to the present, the earth has experienced general warming, and the industrial era is suspect in this regard. Between 1990 and 2006, ten of the warmest years in the last hundred years and possibly since the Little Climatic Optimum occurred. In 2005, we witnessed the warmest global temperatures in the last 1200 years. It was particularly warm in parts of Brazil, North America, northern and southern Africa, Australia, and most of Eurasia.

From the brief description above of earth's climatic history, it is evident that the planet has experienced warmer and colder periods. These shifts in temperature were cycles natural to earth, but human interference is interrupting the natural cycles of temperature to a worrisome extent. Milman (2016) states that Gavin Schmidt, NASA's director of the Goddard Institute for Space Studies, believes that earth is warming at a pace never experienced in the last one thousand years minimum. He says it is very unlikely that increases in global temperatures can be maintained below the 1.5 degree Celsius (34.7 degrees Fahrenheit) mark agreed upon in the Paris Climate Accord of 2016.

To reduce the risks and impacts associated with climate change, a principal goal of the accord is to maintain the increase in the global average temperature to well below 2 degrees Celsius (35.6 degrees Fahrenheit) above preindustrial levels and to take measures to limit temperature increase to 1.5 degrees Celsius (34.7 degrees Fahrenheit) above preindustrial levels.

A January 2017 NASA-NOAA press release said the earth's surface temperature in 2016 was the warmest since such statistics started to be collected in 1880. Average global temperatures in 2016 were 0.99 degrees Celsius (33.7 degrees Fahrenheit) warmer than the mid-twentieth century average; 2016 was the warmest year ever recorded following record-breaking years in 2014 and 2015. That is three consecutive years of record warming; this has never been witnessed since record keeping commenced. The summer of 2018 experienced heat waves around much of the world. North America, Europe, and the Middle East were unusually hot and some say people simply have to begin to get used to hotter temperatures. Left unchecked, temperatures will continue to rise as we have yet to reach a plateau. Sengupta (2018) states, globally 2018 looks as though it will be the fourth-hottest year on record as the first half of the year, not affected by El Niño, was the fourth-warmest on record, according to NOAA. The only years warmer were the three previous ones.

NASA (2018) said earth's average surface temperature has risen about 1.1 degrees Celsius (33.9 degrees Fahrenheit) since the late-nineteenth century. Most of the warming has happened in the last thirty-five years with sixteen of the seventeen warmest years on record occurring since 2001. In relation to this warming, NASA also states that global sea level has already risen about .20 meters (8 inches) since records started being kept in 1880. Projected is an additional rise in sea level at a rate of 3.4 millimeters per annum, or .30–1.2 meters (1–4 feet), by 2100 because of melting land ice and the expansion of seawater as it warms.

NASA also reports that newer projections peg oceanic level rise as high as .20–2.0 meters (.66–6.6 feet) by 2100. Mooney (2018) explains that 2017 was the second-warmest year in recorded history according to NASA, making the past four years the hottest period since record keeping began in 1880. In fact, 2017 proved to be the warmest year on record that was not subject to the El Niño effect, which periodically releases additional heat energy into the atmosphere from the Pacific Ocean and was present in the record warm years of 2015 and 2016.

Is there cause for concern? Samenow published the article "North Pole Surges Above Freezing in the Dead of Winter, Stunning Scientists" in 2018. Though there are parts of the earth that are cold or experience seasonally cold weather, overall, average global temperatures are rising. Many in the scientific community now believe the warmer temperatures of the twentieth and twenty-first centuries are attributable to human enhancement of the earth's greenhouse effect. A significant proportion of the global population, however, is still not convinced that global climatic change is occurring.

The change in world climatic conditions is intricately tied with the Anthropocene epoch. Climate change is a leading representation of environmentally threatening human activity on earth. The first warnings of accelerated and irreversible global warming came from Soviet and US scientists in the 1960s.

There is a lot of science behind the phenomenon of climate change, but the intent of this next section is not to describe all the intricate scientific factors that make up climate change; rather, it is meant to shed light on the general causes and effects.

Earth naturally maintains its own temperature thermostat that varies considerably between different areas of the globe. There exists an intricate relationship between the sun, the atmosphere, and land, water, snow, and ice that creates a balance for the world climate we experience. In the world of earth science, it is described as an energy budget in which incoming solar energy (insolation) radiates heat energy toward the earth, and in turn, a percentage of that total energy is absorbed by specific elements in the atmosphere and on earth such as paved roads, building concrete, and black tarred roofs that absorb heat—the black body effect. Because of the albedo effect, another percentage of the sun's heat is reflected back to space by elements in the atmosphere including clouds, and on the surface of the earth, water, trees and other vegetation, snow, and ice generate a cooling effect.

The earth as a whole is neither gaining nor losing heat energy. When the delicate energy budget is disturbed and no longer in balance, change in world climatic conditions occurs, and it doesn't take very much to cause an imbalance just as it doesn't take much at times for someone's personal financial situation to get out of balance if bills exceed income. We are presently confronted with a continually unbalanced energy budget causing a warming effect referred to as climate change; something is causing the planet to warm. It is widely acknowledged that anthropogenic activity is inadvertently generating the excess heat.

Humankind has altered the natural environment significantly on local, regional, and global levels. The lower atmosphere acts as a natural blanket over the earth's surface maintaining temperature at hospitable levels. This is a natural greenhouse effect; however, human activities such as industrialization are multiplying the natural greenhouse effect, and that is leading to higher global temperatures. Humans are increasing atmospheric concentrations of carbon dioxide by burning wood, coal, oil, and natural gas. Water vapor, dust, methane, and nitrous oxide as well as gases such as halocarbons and aerosols are also very important culprits.

Urbanization has definitely changed climate because, as stated earlier, the physical properties involved, principally concrete, asphalt, and black-tar or membrane rooftops, are absorbers of the sun's heat energy and therefore cause a warming effect. The fact that there are fewer trees in urban areas also contributes to the warming effect because less foliage from vegetation means less reflection of the sun's energy back into space.

Another contributor to the warming effect is widespread deforestation, especially in the tropical rainforests of Brazil, Indonesia, and Zaire. Such reduction of foliage worldwide causes a warming effect on earth because heat energy is absorbed by the ground and human alterations to the ground and is not reflected back into space. Closely related, the general warming effect on the surface of the earth has caused oceans to become warmer because water is an absorber of solar energy, and that further contributes to warmer global temperatures and the melting of polar ice caps, glaciers, and permafrost areas.

Warmer oceanic and river waters mean melting ice and the thermal expansion of bodies of water; both translate into sea level rise and the probable eventual inundation of shorelines that can affect human settlements and activities. A global temperature change of only 2 degrees Celsius (35.6 degrees Fahrenheit) can cause low-lying, small island-nations such as the Maldives in South Asia to be submerged.

In 2016, Australian researchers from the University of Queensland announced that five of the Solomon Islands had disappeared due to a rise in sea level brought on by climate change (Hirla 2016). Samoa in the South Pacific, the Fiji Islands, and the Marshall Islands of the

Pacific are among the many small island-nations that are increasingly threatened by rising sea levels. Highly populated Asian coastal cities will be heavily impacted as well as Australia and the European continent. Over the next centuries, according to Green (2017), cities such as Los Angeles, San Francisco, New York, Boston, and Miami will be threatened by rising sea levels; parts of their shorelines will be flooded or permanently flooded and entire cities or parts of them will be submerged. Major cities such as Chicago and Washington, DC, located along rivers, will not be exempt.

Warmer ocean water also means more-frequent and fiercer hurricanes causing unprecedented disasters. Hurricane Harvey, which hit parts of Texas, and Hurricane Irma, which hit large parts of the Caribbean in 2017, are prime examples. A Canadian Press article (2017) says Hurricane Irma was the strongest Atlantic Ocean storm ever recorded north of the Caribbean and east of the Gulf of Mexico. It happened to spawn at a time when the ocean's temperature was 1 degree Celsius (33.8 degrees Fahrenheit) warmer than usual causing maximum sustained winds of 295 kilometers per hour (183 miles per hour).

Warm water is fuel for hurricanes, and so are higher levels of water vapor in the atmosphere, which human activity is raising in the earth's atmosphere. Is this a sign of things to come? More extreme global weather events such as storms, forest fires, heat waves, droughts, and flooding and in more-intense and new ways are expected. All around the world there is also the very high risk of animal and plant life on land and in the seas that will be affected in terms of distribution and lifecycles as well as loss of habitat and species extinction, not to mention the negative impact of expected drier soils on agriculture.

Strangely, even as climatic change unfurls, some areas and populations of the world stand to gain while others will lose. A longer agricultural season in Canada will make farmers there happy, but ski resort owners may completely lose their seasons.

Rotman (2017) states that Solomon Hsiang, a professor at the Goldman School of Public Policy at Berkeley, concluded that overall, the world's economic productivity will be negatively impacted by warmer global temperatures because people will be less efficient or simply work less. This will affect already warm and poorer countries in particular in South America and Africa, and that will further widen the gap between rich and poor countries. More wealth from poor countries will find its way to the advanced world, including a few northern countries including Russia and most of Europe. It was also concluded that at the social level, hot temperatures increase violence and mortality.

Some of the literature states that by 2100, we may reach 6 degrees Celsius (42.8 degrees Fahrenheit) warmer than today. Carrington (2013) says scientific research indicates that if greenhouse gas emissions are left unchecked, the planet can become minimum 4 degrees Celsius (39.2 degrees Fahrenheit) warmer by 2100. Predictions are that a .5–2 degree Celsius (32.9–35.6

degrees Fahrenheit) increase in global temperature will occur by 2050. If the present rate of greenhouse gas emissions is maintained, the 1.5 degree Celsius (34.7 degrees Fahrenheit) mark could be crossed between 2025 and 2030. A 2 degree Celsius (35.6 degrees Fahrenheit) rise in temperature is sufficient to produce an ice-free Arctic Ocean, and we won't return to the weather of the present. The 2 degree Celsius (35.6 degrees Fahrenheit) mark is therefore a very important marker because it is considered a threshold not to be surpassed. Reaching the 2 degree Celsius (35.6 degrees Fahrenheit) mark is considered dangerous, but going beyond this mark is considered catastrophic.

This is why global leaders met in New York in 2016 to sign what is called the Paris Climate Accord, which officially went into effect on November 4, 2016. The agreement was to limit worldwide greenhouse gas emissions to avoid surpassing the 2 degree Celsius (35.6 degrees Fahrenheit) mark above preindustrial levels. Agreements between 195 world governments focus on decreasing greenhouse emissions so that the rise in temperature does not surpass the safer 1.5 degree Celsius (34.7 degrees Fahrenheit) point. Each participant country voluntarily pursues its own reduction in emissions in line with the goals of the accord, and every five years, they will report results to the United Nations Framework Convention on Climate Change regarding greenhouse gas emissions, mitigation, adaptation, and finance.

There is no enforcement or penalty for not reaching

individually established reduction targets. Parties can report to each other and to the public. If deemed necessary, the countries can modify their plans to reach their targets. It cannot be said at this time that governments have succeeded in hitting their targets in the reduction of greenhouse gases.

The previous major effort at stabilizing global greenhouse emissions was the Kyoto Protocol, which was adopted in Kyoto, Japan, on December 11, 1997, and went into effect on February 16, 2005. It originated from the Rio Earth Summit of 1992 under the United Nations Framework Convention on Climate Change to stabilize global greenhouse emissions. The results were largely unsuccessful. Government leaders signed the protocol in Kyoto, but eventually, major contributors to global gas emissions did not partake in the effort, namely the United States, China, India, and Brazil—citing negative economic impacts to their nations. Canada eventually withdrew from the protocol in December 2012. Without the participation of key nations that are leading contributors to global warming, greenhouse gas emissions continued to rise significantly. The thirty-seven nations that decided to respect the protocol succeeded in reaching emission-reduction targets, but the lack of participation on the part of many key countries caused the demise of the protocol.

Even if greenhouse emissions are brought to near zero in this century, a warmer climate and its effects on the ecosystem and sea level will persist for centuries. How long will the effects of global warming be felt? That depends on how much heat-absorbent gases continue to be emitted into the atmosphere and how sensitive the earth's climatic system is to these emissions because the gases last a long time. Sea levels will rise for many centuries because the oceans take an extremely long time to react to warmer earth surface temperature. Ocean waters will therefore continue warming and sea levels will continue to rise for many centuries at rates equal to or higher than those of the current century. This is why many scientists claim that climate change is irreversible.

The industrial world's and emerging countries' wishes for greater economic development and growth especially via globalization will only amplify and compound the causes and impacts of climate change. Global climatic change has commenced, and it appears a major reduction in greenhouse gas emissions is desperately needed to curb it.

It takes enormous amounts of resources to keep economies moving forward; will emerging countries adopt more-stringent environmental laws to make production and consumption more environmentally friendly? China's massive economic growth in recent decades has not been accompanied by strict environmental regulations. Among other environmental problems, it is confronted with severe air pollution in many major industrial urban areas. This is also the case in India.

# World Overpopulation—Causes and Consequences

A huge stress on the environment is world overpopulation. It took humanity 200,000 years to reach a population of one billion by 1800. Aided by the Industrial Revolution, the population doubled in only 130 years. The third billion emerged in 1959, the fourth billion in 1974, the fifth billion in 1987, and the sixth billion in 1999. We stood at seven billion in 2011 and were at seven and a half billion in 2017. Projections call for the world's population to reach eight billion by 2023 and ten billion by 2056 (Worldmeters 2017).

Population growth has been rising exponentially over the last 218 years, but current annual growth rates and projections show a decline. The world population will continue to grow in the twenty-first century but at a slower rate than in the past.

The rapid growth rate of the world's population over the last 218 years is a result of the difference between the birth rate and the death rate. Historically, infant and child mortality rates were higher and provided a limit to population growth. Today, however, with vast improvements in nutrition, sanitation, and medical care, more children are surviving the important first years of life. A low death rate and a high birth rate lead to rapid population increases in many countries around the world, particularly in Asia, Africa, and Latin America.

This is not only pertinent to children because all segments of populations benefit from advances in nutrition, sanitation, and medicine and are living longer.

Though the amount of food produced has increased in recent decades and public health and medicine have improved around the world, many of these benefits have happened unevenly around the world leaving many still hungry and needing clean water, sewage disposal, and medical care, including vaccinations. Birth rates in less-developed countries remain high in relation to death rates, and that leads to higher population levels. Most of the population increase is occurring in less-developed parts of the world representing three-quarters of humanity. Asia, Africa, and Latin America, characterized as poor, have a less-educated population and larger families. In industrialized nations with more economic prosperity and higher education levels, population growth is slower.

Overpopulation and continual population growth threaten the earth's carrying capacity; it is more than the earth can support. It means elevated use of natural resources by each person, and that is a substantial threat to the environment. Dimick (2014, 10) says we are living beyond our means. He also finds that the wealthier we are and the more educated we are, the more we consume natural resources and energy.

Populous emerging countries such as India and China are becoming more industrialized, and their populations are approaching the West's levels of material consumption. Unlike yesteryear, these countries are now having an impact on the global environment. Other emerging countries such as Indonesia, Pakistan, Turkey, and Bangladesh are doing the same. Imagine a world in a few decades in which many countries once considered Third World reach the same levels of material consumption and environmental demands of the industrialized world today. Multiply many times the demand on natural resources, and that threatens to become a scenario in which earth will not be able to replenish resources quickly enough. Each person added to the world population puts pressure on resources particularly because most folks are after personal enrichment and experiencing all the pleasures life has to offer rather than living with the long-term goal of protecting and living in harmony with the natural world.

We are witnessing serious shortfalls such as declining fish species and stocks, an important sixth mass extinction of species of plants and animals, and worldwide deforestation and associated soil erosion and degradation, and we are experiencing shortages of fresh water. These are the greatest challenges in human history; there are serious worries about being able to cultivate enough food for an expanding population.

If humanity were to suddenly curb or halt the way it lives, economic development, and mass world population growth, it would take decades or centuries for the global environmental ecosystem to return to a normal, natural state of equilibrium.

I draw particular attention to the questions of species threats, endangerment, and extinction. There is clear evidence that the earth's biodiversity is under severe attack and is being lost very quickly. The fifth mass extinction took place sixty-five million years ago when dinosaurs and ammonites existed. Earth's sixth mass extinction is under way. Today, fish, coral reefs, plants, and animals are under attack everywhere. When was the last time you wondered how many rhinos were left in the world or what type of bee is endangered? I would say most people don't worry about such matters. There are simply too many other things in life to put our attention on and certainly many distractions. I was truly taken aback and saddened when I understood the severity of this problem, which hit me like a brick. Just think about it—numerous plants, animals, and marine life we know of may not be around for much longer. Carrington (2017) describes it as a "biological annihilation" of wildlife, and humans are largely responsible for it.

The biggest threat to species stemming from human activity is the destruction of habitats. Aside from the destruction of habitats to accommodate agricultural activities on large tracts of land, habitat destruction also takes place to accommodate sprawling urbanization entailing the destruction of swamps and marshland. Urbanization also entails the damming of rivers and deforestation to build roads, housing, and other structures and facilities. Oil spills, acid precipitation, and water pollution, including aquatic toxicity levels and eutrophication, can negatively impact fish and birds. Many animals are simply overhunted or poached for their meat, fur, or other valuable parts such as ivory tusks.

Many plants and animals are threatened because of the introduction of foreign species from other habitats that bring with them diseases indigenous species can't fight, or they are simply preyed upon by the newly introduced species. Climate change also threatens species. However, the underlying reason is human overpopulation and continued population increase and associated overconsumption particularly by the wealthy.

Hundreds of species are endangered or critically endangered. According to the World Wildlife Fund (2017), among them are Kenya's black rhino; Indonesia's gavan rhino; the amur leopard in the Russian Far East; the Sumatran elephant of Borneo and Sumatra; the Sumatran tiger on Sumatra Island; the saola in Vietnam; the hawksbill turtle throughout the world's tropical oceans; and the south China tiger now considered functionally extinct. We must add to this list the cross-river gorilla of the Congo Basin; the Malayan tiger in the southern tip of Thailand and the Malay peninsula; the blue whale of Southern Chile, the Gulf of California, and the Coral Triangle; the Ganges River dolphin in fresh water Nepal, India, and Bangladesh; and the red panda of the Eastern Himalayas. Other sources reveal that the angel shark of the northeastern Atlantic Ocean; the Russian sturgeon of the Black and Caspian Seas; the Philippine crocodile; and the staghorn coral in Atlantic waters, the Great Barrier Reef, the western coast of South America, and Southeast Asia are also endangered.

# Rising Levels of World Urbanization

Civilization is now experiencing a new historical trend as humans are increasingly concentrated in huge urban areas. The world is now in the urban age. Industrialization, urbanization, globalization, and associated environmental problems are all closely related to each other. The rising level of globalization in particular is spurring this trend.

According to the United Nations World Population Prospects report of 2015 (in Braungardt 2017), globally, more people reside in urban areas than in rural settings. In 2014, 54 percent of the world's population was urban compared to 30 percent in 1950. It is expected that by 2050, 66 percent of the world population will be living in cities. Brown et al. (1999, 40) state that by 2050, six and a half billion people will be living in cities. That is almost equivalent to the total world population of 2017. Braungardt (2017) says that 5 percent of the earth's landmass is used by urban areas; these areas generate about 70 percent of global energy resource consumption and greenhouse gas emissions. He says that rising world urbanization is not happening in developed countries but in emerging and developing countries. Continuing urbanization and population growth in these cities will add two and a half billion people to urban areas by 2050, and 90 percent of the increase will occur in Asia and Africa. It is projected that India, China, and Nigeria alone will produce 37 percent of the world's urban population growth between 2014 and 2050.

Tied to the expected urban population growth of emerging countries is a better standard of living for more people, but that translates into a greater demand for and consumption of goods and services. Amplified levels of global environmental degradation will ensue if the current level of development continues. The physical growth of cities and their populations will contribute to more world environmental degradation, and that will induce more-severe levels of natural disasters originating from tsunamis and flooding because of the elimination of protective natural barriers along rivers, deltas, and coastlines. It will also cause more loss of habitat for plants and animals elevating the threat to and extinction of flora and fauna.

The mass concentration of people in urban areas entails more water pollution because more rural agriculture using chemical technology will be required to feed them, and that will cause more eutrophication and toxicity of waters affecting aquatic life and the marine ecosystem. It also means more urban storm-water runoff mixed with untreated wastewater that will further contribute to poor water quality in the receiving bodies of water.

The lack of basic water treatment in African cities is turning many receiving bodies of water into sewers. Chinese cities are not exempt as many of its rivers do not meet quality standards for safe human consumption. Higher levels of population in cities will also affect the quality of air as more production from factories will be required to supply advanced, emerging, and frontier markets. More household demand for everything will arise, including fresh water, which is already in short supply around the world for many.

With reference to fresh water supplies, according to Brown et al. (1999), rivers such as the Nile in Egypt, the Yellow in China, and the Colorado in the US and Mexico have significantly less water than in the past when emptying into the sea. Water tables are in fact presently decreasing on all continents, including major food-producing regions. Aquifers are also being emptied in the American southern Great Plains, the North China Plain, and in most parts of India. The International Water Management Institute (1998) projects that 1.8 billion people will be living in countries or regions facing fresh water scarcity by 2025. Affected countries will have to reduce the use of water for agricultural purposes, which accounts for 70 percent of fresh water use, to furnish residential and industrial water demands.

China and India, two countries that together dominate the world's irrigated agriculture, will soon be required to substantially decrease the amount of water they use for agricultural purposes. The majority of countries in the Middle East and North Africa are considered to have absolute water scarcity today, and that includes Egypt, Israel, Somalia, Libya, and Yemen. By 2025, Pakistan, South Africa, and large parts of India and China will also be considered as such.

More recent estimates conclude that the number of people affected worldwide by this situation is actually substantially greater than initially thought. A global water crisis is at hand; it is a very serious problem. We will witness countries and regions having conflicts and possibly wars over water—blue gold. In Second and Third World countries, more people migrating to cities and the resulting elevated birth rate means a greater demand for water. They will require more food, and that will take more irrigation of farmland, aggravating the shortage of water.

Higher levels of urbanization also means more use of the automobile contributing to atmospheric concentration of $CO_2$ from Asian countries in particular where leaded gasoline is still burned, and that adds to greenhouse gases. Wood is widely used for cooking and heating in the developing world in countries such as India and Nepal. Much of this practice occurs in rural areas, but it also takes place in urban areas. Together, that contributes to climate change. And increased economic activity in Asian, Latin American, and African cities will add to the greenhouse effect and climate change.

An additional fear is that population growth, particularly in less-developed parts of the world, will create a scenario of unprecedented levels of high urban populations in Mexico City, Lagos, and other huge metropolitan areas that could cause an increase in urban epidemics and infectious diseases. Examples of this are Ebola and Zika that in recent years posed a threat to global health security (Berkley 2016).

# Warnings from the Scientific Community

In November 2017, in a signed letter to humanity, fifteen thousand scientists posted online a second dire warning of coming catastrophic circumstances hovering over humankind. According to these scientists, humankind is on a collision course with nature. Based on Bioscience (2017) and Weston (2017), I summarize the letter: human destruction of the natural world will lead to misery and an irretrievably mutilated planet.

The first warning letter was written and signed in 1992 by fifteen hundred scientists forming the Union of Concerned Scientists. It warned of humanity's impact on the world. Twenty-six years later, global scientists view the same environmental problems as even more severe, and they argue that too little has been done. Except for the ozone layer, which has stabilized, all the major threats identified in 1992 have worsened. The union points out that the amount of fresh water available per capita worldwide has decreased by 26 percent. Dead zones—areas of oceans where life cannot be sustained because of pollution and improper levels of biological oxygen stemming from eutrophication—have increased by 75 percent. Nearly three hundred million acres of forested area has been lost to create agricultural land. There has also been continued growth of global carbon emissions and associated important rises in average temperatures. The total number of mammals, reptiles, amphibians, birds, and fish has decreased by 29 percent while the global population has risen by 35 percent.

Uncontrolled population growth, climate change, deforestation, less access to fresh water, and the extinction of species threaten the human species and the earth. Extremely high levels of consumption of precious resources by an exploding world population rooted in desired economic growth is the biggest danger facing humanity (Weston 2017).

An unfortunate example is found in Cape Town, South Africa, the world's first major city to deplete its fresh water supply because of a multiyear drought. Though the water supply is expected to be replenished, the likelihood is that the situation will repeat itself as climate modeling indicates climatic change will bring fewer wet years and more dry years during this millennium. Rationed water may soon become the new norm for this city of four million (Schlanger 2018), and we can expect more such circumstances in other cities.

Even parts of the United States have been affected. California has problems with water shortages caused by drought, but the problem is widespread and expected to worsen in the US according to Ferris and Sullivan (2016). According to the US Government Accountability Office, forty states have identified at least one region expected to experience some degree of water shortage over the next ten years (Kincaid 2015).

Frank Fenner is an eminent Australian scientist and professor emeritus of microbiology at the Australian National University in Canberra. He has authored or coauthored twenty-two books and 290 scientific papers and book chapters, and he has been a contributor to the eradication of smallpox. He believes the human race will be extinct in a hundred years because of the anthropogenic impact on earth during the industrial era—the Anthropocene epoch. He believes that this era is similar to ice ages and comet impacts. He says that climate change is at only its beginning stages but will likely be the cause of our extinction. He also says that an explosion in world population will cause us to overuse natural resources, thus animals and humans will not be able to survive (Edwards 2010).

Famous British astrophysicist Stephen Hawking made a shocking prediction. He predicted that in a hundred years, humans would have to leave earth and reside on Mars in order to survive because of menacing threats for humanity among which were nuclear war, climate change, viral epidemics, and even artificial intelligence. Attempts should be taken to ensure the survival of humans on earth rather than finding refuge elsewhere (Ferard 2017).

Two problems threatening our species are nuclear war and environmental catastrophe (Chomsky and Polk 2013, 13). Countries confirmed as possessing nuclear weapons in 2017 are Russia with 7,000 units, United States with 6,800, France with 300, China with 260, United Kingdom with 215, Pakistan with 140, India with 110, Israel with 80, and North Korea with 10 (Maps of World 2017).

## Possible Solutions

Humanity has had to endure many problems throughout history, and modern concerns are part of that continuum. Solving modern social and environmental problems is simply easier said than done; giving up gambling, smoking, drinking, and using drugs is very difficult for those who have become dependent on them. Imagine restrictions on water consumption, governmental rules causing companies to adopt costly green technologies, or more taxes such as carbon taxes on corporate and private citizens to protect the natural world. Imagine significant government spending to curb environmental problems or to handle crises.

Imagine requiring modern civilization to stop using oil to produce products or energy. Imagine disallowing further urban expansion by restricting the construction of roads and buildings. Imagine governments disallowing the consumption of fish to allow stocks to replenish. Imagine not being allowed to consume meat products because of the large amount of energy resources required to produce and distribute them.

We have become addicted to approaching our sustenance in a certain manner. We are suddenly confronted with having to alter our human behavior, habits, wants, needs, and expectations. Humanity would have to largely reverse its way of thinking from a mostly antiecological approach to one that embraces and protects the natural world. This could mean deep, radical changes in the essence and structure of today's societies and the economy. It entails incredible shifts in our cultures, values, and beliefs. Such a transition could cause pain for certain segments of societies, political friction, confrontations, harsh economic conditions, civil unrest, and even wars.

Born, however, could be a new type of Renaissance in which the direction taken would be good for the environment and all societies. Our civilization is undergoing continual evolution in an attempt to take us to a higher order of being. In our search for a better society, we cannot leave behind protection of the natural environment because it sustains us. Over the last two centuries in particular, science has been a huge contributor to the destructive type of development known today, but the modern scientific community acknowledges this and warns society about the potential disasters looming. The scientific community is now calling for sound change in the manner humans interact with nature.

What fundamental changes would have to take place to solve the problems facing the planet and our species? It appears a worldwide revolution in thinking would have to occur. This would commence in the advanced world to transition into a safer human-earth relationship. We are so taken and blinded by progress and technology that we cease to comprehend their ill side effects. Humanity would have to move from its mind-set of supremacy and its domineering, aggressive, and exploitive stance over the earth, pull away from the disease of the collective mind called wétiko, and promote much greater public awareness of environmental and social problems, including their causes and effects.

We would have to approach the earth with a renewed and enhanced respect and a revived realization that our relationship with earth is very close and that our survival as a species is totally dependent on nature. Our solutions would have to be based on the spirit of holistic thinking.

Significantly more public pressure will have to be put on authorities to generate much more decisive political will, leadership, and action to change the current destructive pattern of world economic development. International politics needs to think more globally and in a more unified manner about environmental issues and put significantly less emphasis on territorial boundaries for the benefit of single countries. Our civilization would have to create progress of a type that is more environmentally and socially sane, including the protection of global cultural diversity.

A priority for humanity is to bring rapid global population growth under control primarily through proper education and family-planning guidance to restrict the current exorbitant demands put on the natural world by its growing population. We would also have to better manage and preserve the globe's biodiversity by protecting and fostering existing terrestrial, marine, fresh water, and aerial habitats and conserve forests and green areas.

Humanity would have to further devise and encourage the use of new green technologies and widely adopt renewable energy sources while phasing out the use of fossil fuels or apply very strictly enforced emission controls globally to help curb the big problem of anthropogenic global climatic change.

The global population, especially in the wealthiest parts of the world, would be required to change certain behaviors and habits and alter or adopt environmental laws that affect nature positively. A decrease in overall consumption of almost everything is also needed to relieve the planet of various pressures on the global environment. The key to this is education and the sensitization of such matters in people's minds over generations.

In addition to stabilization of ozone depletion over the last twenty-five years, there has been advancement in the reduction of extreme poverty and hunger. There has also been a rapid decline in fertility rates in many regions of the world because of better-educated girls and women. There has been an encouraging decrease in the rate of deforestation in some areas and a noticeable embrace of renewable energy. Yet advancements in environmental policies, human behavioral change, and global inequalities is still insufficient (Bioscience November 2017).

Society has acknowledged that it faces pressing social and environmental problems that need to be resolved. Signs of change for the better are evident in the advanced world, but we currently have very lackluster results; we have only scratched the surface. There's lot's to do, and change is taking place at the very slow pace of poured very thick molasses.

# CONCLUSION

Overall, the Western standard of living has definitely improved over the last 518 years, and there has also been somewhat of an improvement in other parts of the world. However, we still have many social and environmental issues to contend with. Emerging nations, frontier markets, and lesser-developed countries are still not in optimal circumstances. The world political-economic order we have come to know over the last 150 or so years in particular has been maintained; Western nations, commencing with the United States, are still very much ahead of the rest of the world in terms of wealth.

Modern globalization spawned in the West and amplified especially by the Nixon administration commencing with his visit to China in 1972 and the subsequent opening of China to the world economic stage has intensified. The Nixon administration significantly contributed to shaping today's global political picture, overall economic growth, impact on cultural diversity, and the natural environment.

In numerous ways, Nixon's colorful statesmanship and foreign policy changed the world and caused the reawakening and rapid rise of China, the thawing of Cold War tensions with the Russians, the containment of Soviet communist expansion, the political unification of Western Europe, the end of American involvement in the Vietnam War, and increased levels of commercial trade and cultural ties between countries. Nixon's efforts also encouraged and intensified globalization and the world economy.

During his presidency, Nixon was often heavily criticized for his economic policies, but forty-six years after his visit to China, the economic ties the two nations forged have contributed to building China into an economic global engine. Commercial trade and direct investment has benefitted America and China. Many emerging countries of the world are today reliant to differing degrees on welcomed commercial trade with China or want to create such ties and contribute further to global connectivity and the economic multiplier effect throughout the world.

The positive economic prospect offered by globalization and the larger global economy has given birth to many emerging and frontier economies wanting to become the next China. This is the opportunity for many such countries to become advanced nation-states. These countries, however, appear to be developing in a manner that overlooks negative societal and environmental consequences. Modern globalization sustained by global economic development and growth threatens humans and the environment alike. Found in this greater threat is a concern for the loss of global cultural diversity and immense pressure on the earth's ability to supply all the resources humanity requires and its capacity to cleanse the negative by-products of human activity.

The world economy is becoming ever so integrated financially, trade-wise, people-wise, and culturally. This amplifies many times over an existing trend that became progressively prominent in the late 1970s and 1980s with Americanization.

Emerging, frontier, and lesser-developed countries believe that they will prosper and improve their standards of living with globalization. In fact, countries such as China, India, and Japan have gained much ground. These and other Second World nations are challenging Western economies and may pose a greater economic threat to the West as they align themselves and form large economic blocs and perhaps creating a new, multipolar, political-economic world order.

The West and emerging economies stand to benefit economically as new borderless markets are opened for both; investment from the West will flow to these countries and vice versa. The West stands to benefit more because of its rising protectionist public policies and the concentration of wealth in the dominant classes of emerging and frontier countries. Though the global economy is expected to become significantly larger benefitting more inhabitants of emerging and frontier countries, in the foreseeable future the stage is set once again for continuance of unequal distribution of wealth in those nations and between Western and emerging, frontier, and lesser-developed countries. Lesser-developed nations in particular stand to fall deeper into economic problems because they will be pushed aside in a world economic order that benefits nations that have the financial and political clout to participate in the newly emerging world economy.

Projected, however, is that by around 2030, the emerging-market economies of Brazil, China, India, Indonesia, Mexico, Russia, and Turkey together will overtake the G-7 economies of Canada, France, Germany, Italy, Japan, the UK, and the United States. Should this become reality, it shall be interesting to see how such a scenario will affect the overall global political and economic picture, especially, the global balance of power. It shall also be interesting to witness where new leading governments will put their priorities on when it comes to social and environmental problems.

Accompanying the new larger globalized economy due to added participation from emerging nations will be changes in their own cultures. A homogenization of the world's peoples is expected to resemble the present dominant world culture of the West, including its weakened spiritual side, cultural crisis, search for identity, transformation, a slew of problems, but also hope. This may translate into less cultural diversity around the world.

As homogenization takes place, civil unrest could arise in parts of the world because of resistance to acculturation. Also anticipated are accrued environmental problems. With much sought after economic growth from all corners of the globe, concerns for the natural world will also grow. We appear to be entering the proposed Anthropocene epoch, a time in which the world environmental system is dictated and impacted by the actions of humankind. Since 1950 in particular, the world has experienced unprecedented exponential economic growth across numerous indicators. This growth has amplified planet-wide concerns for the natural world commencing with inadvertent global climatic change and associated sea level rises, species threats and extinctions, pressure on natural resources, air-water-terrestrial pollution, rapid global population growth, and concentrated mass activity in more and larger urban areas. Should the current path and type of world development continue, it is feared that emerging, frontier, and eventually lesser-developed nations will add significantly to the degradation of the environment. To all of this must be added the constant threat of disaster from nuclear energy production and warfare.

The human species and the planet are threatened. Since 1992, the world scientific community has officially alerted humanity on two occasions with letters stating that key environmental problems have not been resolved and that human-induced irreversible environmental damage will cause human misery.

Governments and global societies need to rethink how they can proceed with worldwide development and economic growth as well as related globalization. The next statement is certainly easier said than done—we may have to reverse the way we think about and proceed with development and growth if we are to remain in harmony with the natural world. There may well be a new Renaissance that focuses on environmentalism and on societal improvement different from that which resulted from the original Renaissance.

Rather than pushing hard on our current formula to reach new heights in Western and global economic development led by technology characterizing industries 4.0 and 5.0 and commercial trade, we may have to temporarily stop, think, and in an aggressive, head-on fashion confront and solve pressing environmental and social problems before we try to reach newer heights in economic growth.

We need a concerted, world-level effort to formulate comprehensive policies that offer a fair distribution of wealth and opportunity and include lesser-developed nations that have little or no chance of partaking in the highly competitive emerging global economy.

We also desperately need to protect the cultural diversity of the world by protecting indigenous societies, and we need to grapple with the huge need to protect the environment. Accomplishing this will require a world economic development organization with powers of policy formulation and enforcement to create a world economic development plan that will assure all global societies will benefit economically and environmentally.

Only deep revolutionary thinking and nonviolent actions can counter the environmental and social problems we face. Only large actions aimed at global improvement can help, not politics based on divisive, nationalistic self-interest based on territorial boundaries. To proceed with a development that is in tune with Mother Earth, we need a much more encompassing and holistic approach. We need to shift our perspective, embrace and protect the environment, and treat all peoples with respect. For some, it may sound extreme, but we have to start thinking that the natural world is just as important as human beings and that economic development and protection of nature go hand in hand. We need to take action immediately.

In spite of the problems we face, a sparkle of hope exists. It is illuminated by the newest generation, whose members seem to be very slowly planting the seeds of a better way of living. They seek the truth and appear to favor the good of the whole world. In comparison to past generations, they have a heightened awareness of food, hygiene, and health. They are willing to incorporate recycling and curbing greenhouse emissions into their daily lives. They consider it cool to embrace the natural environment, an attitude that was considered uncool in the 1970s. They want to help the unfortunate of the world achieve peaceful existences and coexistence.

We also see it with the #MeToo movement that spread all over social media in the fall of 2017 to help bring to the forefront the widespread frequency and impact of sexual assault and harassment of women, especially in the workplace. We also see it in the want of effective gun legislation. This is certainly not an exhaustive coverage of positive generational change, but the direction involved points to the newest generations searching to flourish in a sane society on a nurturing planet.

The problems they will contend with are colossal. Their approach to politics, economic growth, to the peoples of the world, the natural world, and the manner they treat themselves as individuals will have to be somewhat different from what we have become accustomed to. Just as industrialization altered the face of realty, the kind of new thinking the newest generation is engaging in can alter reality again, hence, a new Renaissance. I hope the new, emerging reality will be one of sound health, peace, prosperity, abundance for all, collective peace of mind, respect among peoples and individuals, a safe global environment, and a renewed sense of spirituality and zest for life.

Do coming generations have enough character to make such changes? Since the 1960s at least, generations have voiced their concern for the protection of the environment, but we are still challenged by issues that pose great threat to humankind. It appears that not enough has been done, and the scientific community is ringing the alarm about the many environmental problems left unchecked that threaten all species, including ours. Many social movements and efforts have voiced concern for the improvement of social conditions, but many social problems persist—the status and condition of women, blacks, and indigenous peoples, as well as the maldistribution of world wealth and continuance of the haves and have-nots.

The resolution of environmental and social issues is

confronted by limitations. Young people with positive intentions and attitudes in these regards grow and begin to develop lives for themselves. They become distracted by careers and making something of themselves. They become distracted by creating families and other matters that can take their focus off other important aspects of life. Though they still want a healthy environment and good social conditions, they can lose their steam because they become preoccupied with personal survival and creating happy lives. I am not being cynical here; I am highlighting that our smart and energetic youth must be crucial players in the social and environmental improvements we all seek.

In early January 2018, I interviewed a thinker, my friend and colleague Andrea Lane, a human resource specialist. We discussed her review of a draft of this book. She is an avid reader, and she had read my first book. As she spoke, in a moment of brilliance I would say, she captured in one short statement what I feel embodies the soul of my writings that I want to share. I was quite happily taken aback and stunned by what she beautifully conveyed. I am compelled to immortalize the essence of her sentiment, which brings to light the thoughts in my works to a more cosmic understanding.

I summarize: humans have always been in constant evolution. We have adopted different means to survive and advance. At one time, it was religion, then science, then industrialization, and now economic growth, money, consumerism, and technology, all with side effects. Maybe it is due to our arrogance that we believe we have the solution. Maybe we have forgotten that it is all connected and that we are all connected. The universe existed and healed itself long before human intervention. Perhaps if we can trust in something greater than ourselves and stop interfering with the natural flow of things because of our fears and limited understanding, we can return to a more natural state of well-being. All we need to do is trust, remember our interconnectivity, appreciate life, and allow it to unfold.

Ours is a beautiful and interesting world, but what's wrong with wanting a better one?

# BIBLIOGRAPHY

Andrews, Evan. 2016. "How Ping-Pong Diplomacy Thawed the Cold War." *History*, April 8, 2016. https// www.history.com/news/ping-pong-diplomacy.

Angus, Ian. 2015. "When Did the Anthropocene Begin ... and Why Does it Matter?" *Monthly Review* 67, no. 4 (September 2015).

Bajpai, Prableen. 2018. "The World's Top 20 Economies." *Investopedia*, August 16, 2018, https://www. investopedia.com/insights/worlds-top-economies/.

Berkley, Seth. 2016. "Zika and Ebola: A Taste of Things to Come?" *BBC News*, February 26, 2016.

Bioscience. 2017. "World Scientists' Warning to Humanity: A Second Notice." *Oxford Academic*, November 13, 2017.

Bloomberg News. 2012. "MISTs Topping BRICS as Smaller Markets Outperform." *Financial Advisor*, August 7, 2012.

Braungardt, Jurgen. 2017. "World Urbanization Trends." *Philosophical Explorations*, April 21, 2017, www.brangardt.trialectics.com/projects/geography/world-urbanization-trends/.

Brown, Lester R., Gary Gardner, and Brian Halweil. 1999. "16 Impacts of Population Growth." *Futurist*, February 1999.

Burrascano, Giovanni. 2016. *So This Is Where We Stand? How Western Thinking Has Changed over the Last Five Hundred Years.* Bloomington, IN: iUniverse.

Canadian Press. 2017. "Hurricane Irma Slams Caribbean Islands as Category 5 Storm." *Herald News*, September 6, 2017.

Capra, Fritjof. 1983. *The Turning Point; Science, Society, and the Rising Culture.* New York: Bantam Books.

Carrington, Damian. 2013. "Planet Likely to Warm by 4C by 2100, Scientists Warn." *Guardian*, December 31, 2013.

———. 2016. "The Anthropocene Epoch: Scientists Declare Dawn of Human-Influenced Age." *Guardian*, August 29, 2016.

———. 2017. "Earth's Sixth Mass Extinction Event Under Way, Scientists Warn." *Guardian*, July 10, 2017.

Castree, Noel. 2016. "An Official Welcome to the Anthropocene Epoch: Scientists Declare a New Age of Humanity." *Rawstory*, August 30, 2016.

Chakravorti, Bhaskar. 2017. "The Next Big Thing: A Fifth Industrial Revolution." *Huffington Post*, February 8, 2017.

Chang, Gordon H. 2015. *Fateful Ties; A History of America's Preoccupation with China*. Cambridge, MA, and London: Harvard University Press.

Chomsky, Noam, and L. Polk. 2013. *Nuclear War and Environmental Catastrophe*. New York: Seven Stories Press.

Cipolla, Carlo M. 1993. *Before the Industrial Revolution: European Society and Economy 1000–1700*. London: Routledge.

Dimick, Dennis. 2014. "As World's Population Booms, Will Its Resources Be Enough for Us?" *National Geographic*, September 21, 2014.

Dobbs, R., J. Manyika, and J. Woetzel. 2015. "The Four Global Forces Breaking All the Trends." Published by McKinsey Global Institute, April, 2015.

Eckersley, Richard. 2012. "Whatever Happened to Western Civilization?" *Futurist*, November–December 2012, http://www.richardeckersley.com.au/attachments/Futurist cultural crisis 2012.pdf.

*Economist*. 2013. "When Giants Slow Down." July 27, 2013. Retrieved online October 24, 2016.

Edwards, Lin. 2010. "Humans Will Be Extinct in 100 Years Says Eminent Scientist." PhysOrg.com, June 23, 2010.

Ernest & Young. 2013. "Hitting the Sweet Spot: The Growth of the Middle Class in Emerging Markets." Skolkovo Business School.

Ferard, Émeline. 2017. "Selon Stephen Hawking, les humains devront quitter la Terre d'ici 100 ans pour survivre." *Gent Side*, Émeline Ferard, May 10, 2017.

Ferris, Sarah, and Peter Sullivan. 2016. "Clean Water Crisis Threatens US." *Hill*, April 25, 2016.

Forbes, Jack D. 2008. *Columbus and Other Cannibals*. New York: Seven Stories Press.

Foster Bellamy, John. 2015. In "When Did the Anthropocene Begin … and Why Does it Matter?" by Ian Angus. *Monthly Review* 67, no. 4 (September 2015).

FTSE Group. 2016. "FTSE Classification of Markets."
September 19, 2016 (retrieved online July 17, 2017).

Gallup. George. 1972. "President Nixon's Popularity
Now At Highest Point in 14 Months." *The Gallup
Poll*, March 9, 1972.

Green, Jared. 2017. "New Map Shows the Impact of
Future Sea Level Rise." *The Dirt-Uniting the Built
& Natural Environments*, January 28, 2017.

Hawksworth, J., H. Audino, and R. Clarry. 2017.
"The Long View: How Will the Global Economic
Order Change by 2050?" PricewaterhouseCoopers,
February 2017.

Hershberg, James G. 1995–96. "The Cold War in
Asia." Edited by James G. Hershberg, *Cold War
International History Project Bulletin*, no. 6–7
(Winter 1995/96), Woodrow Wilson International
Center for Scholars, Washington, DC.

Hirla, Josh. 2016. "Five Islands Have Disappeared Into
the Pacific Ocean, and Six More are Following Suit."
*Science Alert*, May 10, 2016.

Ignatius, David. 2012. "Nixon's Great Decision on
China, 40 Years Later." *Washington Post*, February
10, 2012.

International Water Management Institute. 1998. "Projected Water Scarcity in 2025" IWMI. www. waternunc.com/gb/pws2025.htm.

Kincaid, Ellie. 2015. "California Isn't the Only State With Water Problems." *Business Insider*, April 21, 2015.

Kospanos, Vasileios. 2017. "Industry 5.0—Far From Science Fiction" Part 2." PNMSOFT blog, February 2, 2017.

Lane, Andrea. Personal interview held on January 8, 2018. Montréal, Québec, Canada.

Li, Hongshan, and H. Zhaohui. 1998. *Image, Perception and the Making of U.S.-China Relations*. Lanham, Maryland: University Press of America, p. 403.

Maps of World. 2017. "Countries with Nuclear Weapons." https://www.mapsofworld.com/world-top-ten/world-top-ten-countries-by-nuclear-warheads-map.html. Retrieved online March 30, 2018.

Marsh, Peter. 2012. *The New Industrial Revolution: Consumers, Globalization and the End of Mass Production*. New Haven, CT: Yale University Press.

May, Rollo. 1981. *Man's Search for Himself.* New York: Dell.

McKinsey Global Institute. 2012. "Urban World: Cities and the Rise of the Consuming Class." McKinsey Global Institute, July 17, 2012.

McMurty, John. 1999. *The Cancer Stage of Capitalism: From Crisis to Cure*. London: Pluto Press.

Milman, Oliver. 2016. "NASA: Earth is Warming at a Pace Unprecedented in 1,000 Years." *Guardian*, August 30, 2016.

Mooney, Chris. 2018. "2017 Was among the Planet's Hottest Years on Record, Government Scientists Report." *Chicago Tribune*, January 18, 2018.

Morrison, Wayne M. 2018. "China-U.S. Trade Issues." Congressional Research Service Report, July 30, 2018.

NASA. "Global Climate Change-Vital Signs of the Planet." NASA website https://climate.nasa.gov/effects/. Retrieved January 21, 2018.

NASA-NOAA. "NASA-NOAA Data Show 2016 Warmest Year on Record Globally." NASA-NOAA press release, January 18, 2017.

O'Neill, Jim. 2001. "Building Better Global Economic BRICS." Goldman Sachs Global Economics Paper 66, November 30, 2001.

Pidwirny, M. 2006. "Earth's Climate History." *Fundamentals of Physical Geography*, chap. 7, "Introduction to the Atmosphere," www.physicalgeography.net/fundamentals/chapter7.html. Retrieved online January 21, 2018.

Rotman, David. 2017. "Climate Change is Going to be Very Bad for the Global Economy." *Business Insider*, January 1, 2017.

Samenow, Jason. 2018. "North Pole Surges Above Freezing in the Dead of Winter, Stunning Scientists." *Washington Post*, February 26, 2018.

Schaeffer, Robert K. 2009. *Understanding Globalization; The Social Consequences of Political, Economic, and Environmental Change*. Lanham, MD: Rowman & Littlefield.

Schlanger, Zoë. 2018. "The World's First Major City to Run Out of Water May Have Just Over Three Months Left." *Quartz Africa*, January 11, 2018.

Schultz, Colin. 2013. "Nixon Prolonged Vietnam War for Political Gain—And Johnson Knew About It, Newly Unclassified Tapes Suggest." *Smithsonian.com*, March 18, 2013.

Sengupta, Somini. 2018. "2018 Is Shaping Up to Be the Fourth-Hottest Year. Yet We're Still Not Prepared for Global Warming." *New York Times*, August 9, 2018.

Siracusa, Joseph M., and Hang Thi Thuy Nguyen. 2018. *Richard M. Nixon and European Integration: A Reappraisal*. Switzerland: Palgrave Macmillan, 1st edition.

Stanke, Jaclyn. 1998. "Stanke on Gaiduk, 'The Soviet Union and the Vietnam War'" Jaclyn Stanke. Review of Gaiduk, Ilya V., *The Soviet Union and the Vietnam War*, 1996. H-Russia, H-Net Reviews. May, 1998. http://www.hnet.org/reviews/showrev.php?id=2056.

Stansberry, Cheryl L. 2007. "The Influence of Christianity on Western Civilization." November 14, 2007, http://crossandquill.com/journey/the-influence-of-christianity-on-western-civilization/.

Strothers, Richard B. 1984. "The Great Tambora Eruption in 1815 and Its Aftermath." *Science* 224 (June 15, 1984): 1191–98. http//absabs.harvard.edu/abs/1984sci ... 224.1191s.

Thornton, Richard C. 1982. *China: A Political History, 1917-1980*. Boulder, Colorado: Westview Press Inc.

Weston, Phoebe. 2017. "Catastrophic Warning About the Fate of Humanity Is Given By 15,000 Scientists Who Claim Human Destruction of the Natural World Will Lead to 'Misery' and 'Irretrievably Mutilated' Planet." *Mailonline*, November 13, 2017.

Wilson, Domenic, and Roopa Purushothaman. 2003. "Dreaming With BRICs: The Path to 2050." *Goldman Sachs*. Global Economics Paper 99, October 1, 2003.

Wilson, Domenic, and Anna Stupnytska. 2007. "The N-11: More Than an Acronym." *Goldman Sachs*. Global Economics Paper 153, March 28, 2007.

Worldmeters. "World Population Clock." http://www.worldmeters.info/world-population/. Retrieved online September 5, 2017.

World Wildlife Fund. www.worldwildlife.org/species. Retrieved online October 24, 2017.